W0081838

Praise for *Theory of Water*

"No writer in recent memory has more thoroughly rearranged my moral compass than Leanne Betasamosake Simpson, and no book brought me more solace than *Theory of Water* . . . [An] essential work on love as methodology, on what it means to stand in solidarity with one another and with the earth that sustains us. This is more than just an imagining of something better, but a reminder that better has always been here, has always been possible. A book of immense regenerative power, by one of the few truly incendiary, indispensable writers working today."

—Omar El Akkad, author of *What Strange Paradise* and *One Day Everyone Will Always Have Been Against This*

"One of the most urgent and necessary books I have read in a long time. Profoundly moving and unflinching, it is a deeply personal and generously expansive meditation on what it means to live in communion with the earth and its inhabitants, living, gone, and still to come. This beautiful book is a gesture of hope to a future that might still be possible, if we heed its lessons."

—Maaza Mengiste, author of *The Shadow King*

"A meditation on water, scale, and relation. Placing her body on the shore, on ice and snow, in water with cattails, bark, bullfrogs and more, Betasamosake Simpson . . . demonstrates that 'what we do on a small scale is how we exist at the large scale.' She gives us the word sintering—which is what snow-flakes do to bond in place. It is joining and deformation; it is transformation; it is an ethic of how to live. Sintering should be in all our vocabularies for how to see and imagine each other's linked presences in the world."

—Christina Sharpe, author of *Ordinary Notes*

"*Theory of Water* is a profound, beautifully made work of liberation by a writer deeply attuned to what matters in this world, how to listen to it, how to preserve it, and how to reframe our relationships to reflect it. This is not a book; it is a gift: we are lucky to have it."

—Preti Taneja, author of *We That Are Young*

"Karl Marx wrote, 'To be radical is to grasp the root of the matter'; for him, that matter is man. Leanne Betasamosake Simpson tells us that to be radical is to grasp the *source* of the matter: water. She is right, and she shows us why in this poignant and poetic meditation on the power of water as *Life*. The first victim of colonial/capitalist exploitation, water is also the first line of defense, and our most important site of (re)creation. If we are serious about decolonization, we need a theory of water."

—Robin D. G. Kelley, author of *Freedom Dreams: The Black Radical Imagination*

"In *Theory of Water*, Leanne Betasamosake Simpson moves much like her subject and inspiration—with fluidity as much as force, without fixity yet with steadiness and direction. Asking us to learn from the water that is inside us and between us, Simpson recovers indigenous knowledges that connect past and future but circumvent colonial histories. To make the world again, we are invited to decenter ourselves and

join the flow. A powerful contribution to organizing and to being."
—Gina Dent, co-author of *Abolition. Feminism. Now*

"*Theory of Water* builds a case for deep relationality. Rather than a law-like form of kinship, or model and theory of interdependence, or an account of transactions apportioning material and social worlds, this is a leaky, boundary defying, and rich account of how we come into being through water and *sinter;* how we attach to, and stay alive with this crucial, transitional, and shifting fractal form. Grounded in Anishinaabe thought and history Simpson scales up from the fractal to offer us a theory and model also of internationalism, of social and political intercommunions and permeability occasioned also by water, as mode of transport, as a connector of worlds, regions, life forms. This is a model of Indigenous political thought that refuses all enclosures. *Theory of Water* enacts an intellectual and political history and diplomacy of the present that calls for shared journeys and shared futures."
—Audra Simpson, author of *Mohawk Interruptus: Political Life Across the Borders of Settler States*

"*Theory of Water* offers quiet meditations on what it means to believe in water, Nibi. Water has its own time, ontology, and theory and practice of change. If we listen carefully, as Simpson does, it can teach us to be patient. The transformations of water from solid to liquid to gas are sometimes quick, like snow melting in the Spring, and at other times unfold over countless generations, like a glacier carving its way across the land. The answers water provides are healing, regenerative, and flowing in ways that breach and dissolve the rigid social hierarchies of colonialism and capitalism. Simpson asks herself and the reader, Do you believe in water?"

—Nick Estes, author of *Our History Is the Future: Standing Rock Versus the Dakota Access Pipeline, and the Long Tradition of Indigenous Resistance*

"'Love is the necessary precursor to world building,' Leanne Betasamosake Simpson teaches us, before she proceeds to enact that very idea with a fierce generosity in this book. *Theory of Water* offers us new ways of relating to that animating spirit that keeps us alive, that binds us together in shared fate. Water is teacher, water is ancestor, water is power, and water is song. Through tender moments of mourning an Elder and unapologetic assertions of rage at colonial injustice, Simpson offers a tremendous gift for those seeking a shared map for reciprocity, accountability, and resilience."

—Eve L. Ewing, author of *Original Sins*

"A beautiful, meditative, and clear-eyed reflection on our shared life on a fragile planet hurtling towards a precipice— one brought about by rapacious colonialism and its attendant systems of exploitation. Leanne Simpson's *Theory of Water* is an origin story, a prayer, and a call to action for an inter-connected, sintered way of life. The 'sound of rushing water' transported me to my homeland in Kashmir where 'water on land, land on water' as an age-old mode of living is now under threat from extractive development. Everybody should read this profound book."

—Mirza Waheed, author of *The Collaborator*

theory of water

Also by
Leanne Betasamosake Simpson

Rehearsals for Living (coauthored with Robyn Maynard)

A Short History of the Blockade: Giant Beavers, Diplomacy,
and Regeneration in Nishnaabewan

Noopiming: The Cure for White Ladies

As We Have Always Done: Indigenous Freedom
Through Radical Resistance

This Accident of Being Lost

Islands of Decolonial Love: Stories & Songs

Dancing on Our Turtle's Back: Stories of Nishnaabeg Re-Creation,
Resurgence and a New Emergence

The Gift is in the Making: Anishnaabeg Stories

LEANNE BETASAMOSAKE SIMPSON

theory of water

NISHNAABE MAPS
TO THE TIMES
AHEAD

ALCHEMY
BY KNOPF CANADA

Copyright © 2025 Leanne Betasamosake Simpson

All rights reserved. No part of this book may be reproduced, scanned, transmitted, or distributed in any form or by any electronic or mechanical means, including information storage and retrieval systems, without permission in writing from the publisher, except by a reviewer, who may quote brief passages in a review. No part of this book may be used or reproduced in any manner for the purpose of training artificial intelligence technologies or systems. Published in 2025 by Alchemy by Knopf Canada, a line of books within Alfred A. Knopf Canada, a division of Penguin Random House Canada Limited, Toronto.

Knopf Canada
Penguin Random House Canada
320 Front Street West, Suite 1400
Toronto, Ontario, M5V 3B6, Canada

penguinrandomhouse.ca

Alchemy by Knopf Canada and colophon are registered trademarks.

The authorized representative in the EU for product safety and compliance is Penguin Random House Ireland, Morrison Chambers, 32 Nassau Street, Dublin D02 YH68, Ireland, https://eu-contact.penguin.ie

Library and Archives Canada Cataloguing in Publication
Title: Theory of water / Leanne Betasamosake Simpson.
Names: Simpson, Leanne Betasamosake, 1971- author.
Identifiers: Canadiana (print) 20240410335 | Canadiana (ebook) 20240418328 |
ISBN 9781039010246 (hardcover) |
ISBN 9781039010253 (EPUB)
Subjects: LCSH: Water—Philosophy. | LCSH: Water—History. |
LCSH: Water—Social aspects. |
LCSH: Water and civilization. | CSH: Ojibway.
Classification: LCC BF789.W3 S56 2025 | DDC 553.701—dc23

Text design: Kelly Hill
Cover design: Kelly Hill
Cover image: Water Study © Christi Belcourt
Typeset by: Kianna Mkhonza

Printed in the United States of America

3rd Printing

ALCHEMY
BY KNOPF CANADA

Penguin
Random House
Canada

To Gidigaa Migizi ban
1942–2022

Contents

When It Was Icy, I Could Fly

My collaborators on this book were snow and ice, slush and rain. I would get up before sunrise in the winter, which isn't that difficult where I live, and write. And then I would either groom the nearby ski trail, skate-ski or both. Every day. When I could no longer write, I skied. On the trail, my brain made connections and found ideas that it couldn't make or find when I was sitting in front of a computer screen. All my thinking was done on that trail, sometimes when my skis were slow and the snow was fresh and cold, and the demands on my body were the greatest; sometimes when it was near zero and the snow was hard-packed; and sometimes when it was icy, and I could fly.

I've skied for as long as I can remember. My parents took a photo of me at two years old in my first pair of skis, plastic blue Super Slider Snow-Skates. I can remember every pair of skis I've owned, and I still use the first pair of skating skis I bought when I was sixteen. I ski if it is at all possible to do so. In blizzards and in rain—and even when there isn't enough snow left to ski without stopping, I ski and portage. When it is absolutely impossible to do this, I run along the same trail, dreaming of skiing.

Even so, it wasn't until several years ago that I first paid close attention to water and all its transformations. For more than a month one spring, I witnessed a lake in the Northwest Territories melting from ice into water in the spring. Every day was different. Every hour was different. The sounds of ice breaking were unlike any other sounds I'd ever heard. I saw how the people and animals living on the shore of the lake continually adapted to the state of the lake. During breakup, the lake is their focus, and it is constantly changing.

I made a record of that thinking and experience in an album called *Theory of Ice*. Normally, playing the songs by touring with my band would have deepened my understanding of the album. The rehearsals, the repetition, the playing to different audiences in different places. The pandemic truncated all that. We barely played *Theory of Ice*.

But even when the record was long released, I couldn't stop thinking about theories of ice, theories of snow, theories of water.

Skiing depends on those understandings.

Skiing is not a particularly Nishnaabeg practice. I say "particularly" because there must have been some Nishnaabeg in the past, unknown to me, who strapped boards or bark to their feet and slid across the snow. The word for toboggan comes from our word *zhooshkodaabaan*: *zhoosh* meaning smooth or slippery, and *daabaan* meaning vehicle or sled.[1] Skiing is, however, widely known to be part of a Sami way of living. Like most Indigenous practices, it was primarily utilitarian: sometimes, and in some conditions, skiing is a fast way to travel in the winter.

When I was a kid, I remember watching Sharon and Shirley Firth, Gwich'in members of the Canadian Cross

Country Ski Team at the 1980 Olympics in Lake Placid. It was their second Olympics and eventually I would watch them race a third time, in 1984 at Sarajevo. I remember their long dark braids.

In June 2021, during the pandemic, instead of a large gathering, the annual meeting of the Native American and Indigenous Studies Association was marked by several smaller regional gatherings. My colleagues and I hosted one of these at the Yellowknife Ski Club, near the northern boundary of the city. The chalet was perfect for our purposes. It had a kitchen, a meeting space, an outdoor space and lots of windows and doors to open for good air circulation. And on the walls of the main room were framed photographs of competitive skiers from the 1960s, 1970s and 1980s, many of them Dene. I recognized the writer and artist Antoine Mountain, the Elder, journalist and broadcaster Paul Andrew, and of course Shirley and Sharon Firth.

I knew that some of these skiers had been part of the Territorial Experimental Ski Training (TEST) program, which had been created in 1967 in Inuvik "to see how the sport of skiing might contribute to the motivation and success of Indigenous youth navigating a rapidly changing world."[2] The program was started by a French Oblate priest, Father Jean-Marie Mouchet, who had been part of the French Resistance patrolling the French-Italian border on skis. He'd ended up in a Nazi concentration camp before immigrating to Canada to be a priest. Indigenous students in the program came from Grollier Hall, a Catholic hostel, and Stringer Hall, an Anglican hostel, both of which were part of the residential school system.

These hostels were sites of horrific abuse, and while the internet is full of quirky and loving stories about Mouchet,[3] I still can't help but remember that he was there at a time when his colleagues were doing unspeakable things to children.[4] Many of the participants in the TEST program speak of skiing, with its intense cardiovascular and physical demands, and of spending long hours on the land as a flight from residential school. The Dene journalist Paul Andrew wrote: "Skiing provided students with a vital connection to the land—a connection the residential school system, through its removal of children from their families and territories, actively sought to break. For others, it was an escape."[5]

Former student Harold Cook, who spoke openly about the abuse he endured while at Grollier Hall, also described this fugitivity: "'I imagined the abuser being the one ahead of me and I took all of my aggression out on the skis,' he told a group of Aklavik students in 2016, during a speech about the benefit of sports."[6] Angus Cockney was another who found skiing to be an "escape hatch": "For me back then, being in that system, skiing became my escape hatch from the abuse that happened at that school. For me skiing was a way out. I adopted it as a lifestyle and I'm glad my kids did, too."[7]

Now, when I'm on the trail, I think of those kids at residential school, skiing to escape. For me, Father Mouchet isn't the hero in this story; it's those kids, who were able to find themselves in the land, the ice, the snow, and who used this as a fugitive way to dream beyond their present moment.

In the bush, and in snow.

I know this escape hatch. Through it, and through my collaboration with ice and snow, this book came to be.

Nibi

It was in the final chapter of my book *Rehearsals for Living*, as I was writing the last letter to my co-author Robyn Maynard, that I began to think about water, Nibi, as a theory, or a mapping of life and affiliation and global connection— in other words, as a form of Indigenous internationalism. I became interested in thinking alongside water as it travelled the globe over and over, moving inside and outside bodies across all kinds of borders, and as it changed form from solid to liquid to gas. And I remain interested in its continual movement and cycling, its immense relationship with all forms of life on the planet.

Colonialism has forced Indigenous peoples to talk, think and organize around land in our resistance to ongoing dispossession. But within Nishnaabeg culture there are also responsibilities for the caretaking of water, and often these reside in the realm of women or people who give birth. Often in our ceremonies, these people will sing and pray to water, focusing on expressing our communal love, dependency and gratitude for Nibi's life-giving qualities. And some have become activists. From 2003 to 2017, Elder Josephine Mandamin led a movement of water walkers—

people who walked around the Great Lakes, drawing attention to the health and well-being of the water. The activist
Autumn Peltier from Wikwemikong has been fighting for
access to clean drinking water for a decade, since she was
twelve years old. Mohawk midwife Katsi Cook teaches us
that water in our mothers is our first environment, and
the health of the amniotic fluid that surrounds us there is
directly related to the health of the aquifers and lakes that
surround us in the larger world. Meanwhile, Nishnaabeg
fasting ceremonies, which include spending time on the
land in the spring and going for four days and four nights
without water, reinforce the idea that we cannot exist very
long without this element.

All genders and all forms of life have a relationship with
water. Water droplets in our breath connect us intimately, as
we learned during the pandemic. Nishnaabeg think of water
as the lifeblood of the earth. We think of the Great Lakes as
internal organs that filter and clean water before sending it
along the Gchi-Ziibing, or the St. Lawrence River, to the
Atlantic Ocean. In this sense, the health of the Great Lakes
is akin to the health of our own kidneys and liver. We rely
upon coastal peoples to take care of the water in the Arctic,
Pacific and Atlantic Oceans. We rely on northern peoples
to take care of the permafrost, snow and sea ice. We rely on
Indigenous peoples in deserts and arid regions around the
globe to advise us of the great power that even a little bit
of water holds. We rely on mountain peoples to take care
of headwaters and glaciers. In my own practice, I rely on
writers and thinkers like Christina Sharpe and Alexis Pauline
Gumbs to teach me what Black feminists theorize about the
Atlantic and the middle passage.

In the face of ongoing dispossession, Indigenous peoples have written much about the importance of land to our continued existence. Land and land-based practices are the nest within which we learn our philosophies, laws, ethics and politics. And while water is, in this context, considered to be an integral part of the land, I am interested in the theories that water, in and of itself, holds for living, organizing and making worlds beyond the ones we've inherited from colonialism and racial capitalism.

The present moment—one of climate catastrophe, of ongoing genocide and Nakba in Gaza, Palestine, of genocides in Sudan and Congo—demands that we direct our dreams and actions towards making worlds that refuse capitalism and dispossession and the spectacular violences required to maintain them. The present moment demands that we figure out how to create and maintain robust constellations of co-resistance and provide material support for anticolonial movements locally and globally. As the axis of capital, and the states protecting that capital, descend into fascism, the present moment demands that we come together and face our linked crises in a manner that ensures the sanctity of the planet for all species and generations yet to come.

The theory of Nibi asks us to think on a scale that is outside the present moment and our own immediate needs. I'm thinking about Nibi as theory here because Nibi offers us an invitation to learn from its embodied practice, a practice of cycling that is global, is permeable and brings about a continuous rebirth on our planet. Nibi asks us to ground ourselves intimately in land and place, and relate that grounding to other movements, geographies, cultures and lands. The shorelines of our lands, shaped by water,

teach us about fractals—patterns repeated across scales—
and show Nishnaabeg that the same practices we engage in
within our family are the practices we engage in as nations
and in the larger universe. Nibi teaches us that our thinking is most powerful when it can connect the intimate to
the global and move between scales effortlessly. Nibi, water,
is iterative, resilient and transformative as it carves out
spaces from rock over thousands of years. And water, Nibi, is
interdependent and decentralized, a vessel for multitudes of
land- and water-based species and communities. And finally,
water and Nibi always create more possibilities. Water and
Nibi are working within mino-bimaadiziwin to propel a
continuous, global rebirth of life.[8]

Nibi, like all Nishnaabeg theories, is an emergent theory
of internationalism. Nibi's practices on a small scale are
replicated on a larger scale. Nibi works with, and asks us to
embrace, uncertainty, multiplicity, adaptation, iteration and
decentralization, as forces that create the conditions for life
to emerge and continue. Nibi is inside us, and it connects us
to all forms of life on the planet. Nibi matters.

Listening in Our Present Moment

"I do not have day and I do not have moonlight
I do not believe in time
I do believe in water"[9]

In 1991, Rebecca Belmore made a six-by-seven-feet-wide wooden megaphone in response to the so-called "Oka Crisis," a Kanien'kehá:ka uprising to defend their sacred pines and a burial ground from becoming an eighteen-hole golf course. Belmore wanted people to address the land directly, much as our ancestors had, and to experience "political protest as poetic action." The sound installation and mixed media sculpture is large. It is made of plywood, cork, cork inlay, mahogany veneer, varnish, fibreglass, leather and ochre, and embedded with a loud-hailer. It looks like a very large version of a birchbark moose caller, used by hunters to call in moose. Over the next few years, she travelled with the piece, setting it up on reserves, shorelines, sacred places and sites of resistance. Along the way, she often slept beside it in her van. In Anishinaabemowin, the piece was called *Ayum-ee-aawach Oomama-mowan* (translated into English as *Speaking to Their Mother*), and as Belmore travelled, the piece became an instrument invoking a gathering space for Indigenous people to amplify our voices and speak directly to the land.

Our old people, Belmore's and mine, had and have an intimate relationship with the land and the water. They spoke to the sun in the mornings and the moon at night as cherished relatives. They visited with the water lilies and Labrador tea before they picked these plants to make medicine. They prayed to the ones that had passed on to the spirit world, and they prayed to the spiritual beings that lived in their worlds. They spoke with and dreamed of beavers and muskrats before they harvested them. They made offerings to the whitefish before setting nets, and to the lakes and rivers for safe passage. They were in constant dialogue with the living things that made up their world—which is saying something, because Anishinaabe are not known as chatty people. Many Anishinaabe still do this today while harvesting, making medicines or in ceremony. For many of us, the sound waves of our voices, vibrations made from the instrument of the body, are an affecting force in the universe. It is within this context that I understand *Ayum-ee-aawach Oomama-mowan*.

At first, Belmore installed the piece on the land, outside galleries, outside the confines of the so-called white box, and into the network of living things that contains the potentiality of Indigenous peoples. In this way, the performance-installation became a gathering site, a communal meaning-making project and a space that generates knowledge. *Ayum-ee-aawach Oomama-mowan* placed bodies in relation to land and water and asked us to engage through sound and listening. In a conversation with Anishinaabe curator Wanda Nanibush in 2014, Belmore said that her strategy of bringing a conceptual artwork, in the form of a functional tool, to the people and asking them to speak directly to the land itself, as we have always done, strengthened her understanding of the role of the artist: "The 'artist,' the maker, the visionary has always been a part of who we are."[10]

Looking back now at the photographs and the videos from the first journeys of *Ayum-ee-aawach Oomama-mowan*, I get a strong sense of how the piece brought people together. At Fort William First Nation, where the art was facing Lake Superior, and at the Wiggins Bay blockade in northern Saskatchewan, the piece is surrounded by friends, families, children and Elders. There are fires burning and people visiting. There is the sharing of food and stories, and people taking turns speaking through the megaphone. People are embracing the piece, speaking their hearts and minds, their bodies and voices becoming the piece too, becoming part of the multiple meanings it generated.[11]

There are only a few recordings of what Indigenous peoples said into the megaphone. In retrospect, this is a lovely part of the work, and only possible because *Ayum-ee-aawach Oomama-mowan* was born in the 1990s, when we didn't yet record everything on our phones. The thousands of conversations that took place were private and remained between the speakers, those gathered in that spot at the time, and the universe. Rehearsed and unrehearsed, in English, in Anishinaabemowin, in song and prayer: the things that were said and the things that were unsaid, the demotic accounting of lives.[12] A collective accounting of a present moment. The point of the piece was not just the content of the speeches or even the megaphone itself as a piece of conceptual art. Rather, meaning was made through speaking and listening, and through travelling the land, bringing people together to engage in the practice of speaking and listening to non-human forms of life on reserves, in towns and cities, and at sites of Indigenous Land reclamation.

When I think of that piece today, I think of the iconic photo showing it upon our sacred Animikii-wajiw, in the care of Fort William First Nation in Thunder Bay, Ontario. It was installed facing Lake Superior, below where the Animikiig, or Thunderbirds, nest. I imagine what it would have been like to be there that day, the laughing, the joy, the sense of being present. In contrast, I remember my kids being frightened of their own voices as *Ayum-ee-aawach Oomama-mowan* amplified them in the scary white-box gallery of the National Gallery in Ottawa, pointing out how out of place it was there. I think, too, of the birchbark moose cone-callers our hunters use in the fall, which is perhaps the form that this piece enlarges, and the circumstances that compelled Belmore to build a megaphone so that our ancestors and our relatives could hear our voices over the noise of capitalism—noise that has only become louder and more total since the piece was created in the 1990s.

Belmore remembers the first installation of *Ayum-ee-aawach Oomama-mowan* in the mountains of Banff National Park. Inside the megaphone shape, she had placed a battery-operated hailer that amplified the voice of any speaker talking into the sculpture. She talks about how the sound would build and go out into the landscape and onto the land and find an echo. In Banff, this was acoustically amazing, as the speaker's voice would echo nine, ten, eleven times. Belmore says that the point of this piece was to look at the idea of Indigenous protest, and to aim participants' voices not at the government, the prime minister or the army, but at the land itself. The idea was that the land has been hearing the sound of us for a very, very long time.[13] The echo asks the speaker to be confronted with their own self-reflection, between the land and themselves.[14]

I think of our ancestors, who spoke to *their* ancestors through the sound of rushing water. It's one of the many reasons that hydro dams, interpretive centres and lift locks are so irritating to us: they close off channels of communication. The sound of rushing water is a kind of portal to another world. Places where waves of energy altered human hearing were often where spiritual beings lived or where certain significant events happened. And the sounds in these places, such as that of water moving, were normalized. The idea that Belmore would have to stop us and amplify the sounds so we could hear them would be startling to these ancestors.

While the relevance of *Ayum-ee-aawach Oomama-mowan* still resonates today, the work also gave birth to siblings in 2017, in a series called *Wave Sound*. Revisiting and inverting the concept of the megaphone, Belmore made four sculptures, varying in shape and form, to amplify the sound of water and shoreline. The sculptures were installed in Banff National Park, Alberta, Gros Morne National Park in Newfoundland, in Anishinaabe territory at Pukaskwa National Park in Ontario and on reserve at Chimnissing Island in Georgian Bay, which is part of the Beausoleil First Nation in Ontario. Three of the 170-pound conical listening devices were made of aluminum casts, an aesthetic echo of who the listeners were likely to be in the locations where these three were installed: non-Indigenous peoples. For the sculpture on reserve land, Belmore used copper, a material that echoes Anishinaabe history, story and material use. Copper is said to be the blood of two groups of Manidoog, or spirits, Animikiig (Thunderbirds) and Mishibizhiig (the Underwater Panthers), who engaged in an epic battle in the Great Lakes region, spilling their blood on shorelines and rocky outcrops. Copper offers itself to the Anishinaabeg by making itself visible on the ground. It is used to hold water in our ceremonies, and represents spaces in between the sky, waters and land.[15] To make the sculptures, Belmore cast the rock in each site-specific location, rock that was created out of thousands of years of wind, rain, snow and ice, and then wrapped the castings around conical frames. The forms were helicoptered into the sites so that visitors would happen upon them while hiking. These were large-scale, temporary installations, camouflaged in their surrounds, amplifying the unique sounds of each place.[16]

Instead of inviting us to speak, *Wave Sound* asks us to practice embodied listening—a deep listening and feeling using one's entire being. *Wave Sound* is an invitation to gather at the shore, sit down and use our bodies to hear wind, rock, sand—maybe even mosquitoes and the durational rhythm of waves. Iris Blake writes that *Wave Sound* gestures towards listening and disability, with the conical devices functioning as hearing aids.[17] I think that it suggests how settlers under colonialism have never, ever been able to hear the expansive web of living things that we refer to as land, just as they have never heard Indigenous peoples. When I encounter it, even in a gallery setting, I don't *look* at *Wave Sound*—although I could for a long time, because it is aesthetically stunning. Instead, I become *enmeshed* in

Wave Sound, placing my body on the land to quiet it, and to listen beside Nibi, to listen through Nibi, to listen with Nibi—a being that changes form from liquid to solid to gas, that travels the skyworld, the underground, and inside and outside my body, an ancient formation of molecules that has been the same since the beginning of this world. A fugitive that erodes and escapes containment, and one that we simply cannot live without.

I quiet. I listen.

Through these rehearsals, *Wave Sound* for me amplifies the voices of water to cut through the noise of colonialism. It works in concert with my great-grandparents praying and carrying water, and with those yet to be born, to become a practice. Together with my cochlea and auditory nerve, my mind and my heart, *Wave Sound* transforms from instrument to belonging as Nibi, Belmore and all the life she has gathered work alongside me to generate meaning and inspire new worlds.

And so, I take Belmore's invitation seriously. After three years of pandemic, amplified fascism, freedom convoys, dying glaciers, misdiagnoses, police killings, children alone in cages at borders, open-air prisons for entire peoples, all in the name of racial capitalism, I'm asking myself: What does it mean to listen to water?

What does it mean to believe in water?[18]

4

Sintering

Jackson Creek is down the street from where I live in Peter-borough, Ontario. It flows into the man-made Little Lake, then into the Otonabee River and eventually into Lake Ontario. There is a 4.5-kilometre trail alongside the creek where I run in spring, summer, fall and parts of the winter when I can't skate-ski on it. Jackson Creek is, by most accounts, an unremarkable urban creek—I imagine much like every other urban creek in North America. And it is the body of water I spend the most time with every day.

Peterborough is built on top of Jackson Creek, a fact that became evident to most residents in 2004, after more than 150 millimetres of rain fell in less than two hours and the creek burst its banks and flooded the city's downtown. These were the real and poetic consequences of constraining the creek to make room for urban development, forcing it into smaller and smaller underground tunnels unable to carry stormwater, tunnels that instead furiously expelled it without regard for homes, cars or city infrastructure.[19]

Doug Williams, my Elder and friend, who passed away in July 2022, used to talk about the creek and its portage as part of a Michi Saagiig Nishnaabeg route that connected

Nogojiwanong—the place at the foot of the rapids, or Peterborough—with Chemong Lake. Every time I'm on the trail, I think of Doug, and I think of that passageway.[20]

One day recently the creek was beginning to freeze after the first big storm of the winter brought us nearly thirty centimetres of snow. I was up early, on the snowmobile doing passes along the trail, compacting the heavy, wet snow so that tomorrow another driver could attach the groomer. I had started helping groom the trail a year earlier, during one of the pandemic winters. I volunteered at first just to keep up my snowmobile skills when I was in the south so that when I returned to work in the north, I didn't have to relearn how to drive the sled every time. Grooming the trail certainly helped with that, but soon those technical skills were eclipsed by something else entirely.

As a lifelong skier and lover of the winter, I thought I knew a lot about snow. When I was a competitive skier, I spent a lot of time figuring out wax by measuring snow temperature and paying attention to how much water the snow was carrying, how fresh it was and how packed the trail. This is a crucial part of ski racing, and it is why Olympic Nordic teams have waxing coaches and teams of people monitoring the snow. Races are won and lost on waxing. I thought I knew something about it. And I was wrong.

I discovered that nearly every day the snow was slightly different along the trail at Jackson Creek. I became fascinated by sintering. When a snowflake falls from the sky and lands on the earth, it immediately begins, or perhaps continues, a transformation as it forms bonds at temperatures below zero (this is not a melting process) with its neighbouring snowflakes or crystals to create the fabric of a snowpack.

Sintering is a joining. It is a communal transformation that creates a fabric of former snowflakes bonded to each other. It is a process of changing from a singular, angular snowflake to a more rounded form of bonded crystals, or a snowpack— a denser, more compact, linked formation.[21] As the snow sinters, it settles and becomes denser, stronger and soggier under the influence of gravity. Sintering is slow deformation.

Groomers pay attention to sintering because there is nothing like skating along a well-groomed trail of packed snow. It feels like flying.

Many factors influence sintering: temperature, humidity, time of day, weather, who is using the trail and how. But I think of none of those each morning when I'm on the sled. I think only of this idea: that the first thing a snowflake does when it lands from the skyworld is to join bonds, actual physical bonds, with its neighbours.

It weaves itself into its environment, and it does so in a way that doesn't destroy its neighbours.

Sintering is bonding; it is building coalitions with your neighbours.

And these coalitions mean that the packed sinter snow on the trail has staying power, that it remains long after spring has melted the snow around it.

Snowflakes are extraordinary. I understand from snow scientists that they start out as a single nucleated dust particle that attracts water droplets, and that these in turn freeze and accrete into a crystal form. The temperature and humidity in the skyworld mould the snowflake into complex shapes as it moves through the atmosphere. No two are the same as they act en masse and in communion to form magnificent storms, upheavals and blankets.

When I signed up to be a groomer, I was expecting to learn practical things—how to start a tired, aging, cold snowmobile; the correct speed for dragging the groomer utensil over the trail so that it is properly packed; how to back up and turn around while pulling something.

I wasn't expecting the snow to teach me how to live in the world.

But of course, this is why I love the land, and this is why I spend as much time as I do sintering with the lakes and rivers, cedars and maples, deer and geese. The snow is telling me that sintering is how Michi Saagiig Nishnaabeg make worlds, how we weave ourselves into the land without destroying it. A snowstorm reminds me of what radical overturning and transformations can be accomplished when sintering creates deep attachments across many, many individuals. Sintering in the forest is easy for me; sintering with people I'm currently sharing the planet with, much more difficult. These days, I ask myself if sintering could play a role in grounding my method of solidarity, in strengthening and renewing connections across communities of struggle towards new constellations of co-resistance. Could sintering be a foundational concept for creating such constellations?

One early morning while I was grooming the trail, I was thinking about sintering and listening to a podcast called *Conjuncture*. The episode, "Against Pessimism," featured Robin D.G. Kelley,[22] and in it, Robin spoke with Jordan T. Camp about a variety of topics coalescing around our present moment. Robin spoke about this moment that we all share, telling us that liberalism and fascism share the same goals: to shore up capitalism, maintain class and surplus, and keep the markets afloat. Sometimes, he said, fascism works better; at other times, liberalism. Fascism makes liberalism possible. I thought of Justin Trudeau wearing his reconciliation socks, embodying the idea that he is Indigenous peoples' best friend with his tattoo, the smudging, the big drum and blanket, the headdress. Meanwhile, he has whittled colonialism down to residential school abuses; he has paid the money and facilitated the Pope. I imagined Trudeau's team organizing Instagram posts of hide tanning and powwow dancing, logging them into their database and constructing a brand of Indigeneity that is a good sell to liberal whites and liberal Indigenous peoples alike. This anti-racist, multicultural fuel is what financial capital thrives on, as Kelley said to Camp.

In another part of the podcast, Robin talked about Gramsci and his 1924 work *Against Pessimism* ("I am trying to remember all of it," he said, although to me it seemed his mind held an astounding catalogue of details). He talked about how Gramsci pushed back against Communist International and the historic moment when Italian Communists, facing Mussolini's fascist rise, declared, "We have to withdraw." According to Gramsci, this was pessimism defined by fatalism—the idea that the crisis was coming, the economy was about to collapse, and the Communists would just have to wait it out. Gramsci said no. We need to act now. We can't wait. We need worker rebellions like the ones that occurred in Turin.[23]

Listening to this, I wrote down: "This is where we are. We don't need to be defensive about anti-fascism, but active, engaged and on the offensive."

And: "Masses of people in rebellion create the crisis."

I thought about the past few years, our recent history that showed the precarity of life, and also the calculations about who was worthy of living and who was assigned to perish. I thought of the never-ending crises and how it was easy, very easy, for some of us to be disengaged, to just wait it out. I thought about what was happening that very day—which was the day after COP 15 struck its "historic deal" to sacrifice 70 percent of the planet, the day the world waited for the January 6 panel to announce what we already all knew, the day the Dutch prime minister performed an apology for the Netherlands' "historic role in the slave trade." I thought about the ongoing genocides—in Gaza, the Sudan, Congo. And here I was listening to a thinker I deeply respected who compelled me—demanded, even—to be active and on the offensive. Who demanded that I fight, that we fight. That we fight together.

Kelley talked about Cedric Robinson's work as "Black anti-fascism," and I thought about what Indigenous anti-fascism might look like, and Anishinaabeg anti-fascism, Michi Saagiig Nishnaabeg anti-fascism. That is, I wondered, What would it look like to have a critique of fascism from within the formation of thought, and perhaps a specific school of thought, of the Michi Saagiig Nishnaabeg? What would it mean to have the sort of structuring and organizing that occurs outside what we usually imagine when we think of movements and anti-fascist writers and scholarship on these issues? What would it look like to have a school of thought that is largely embodied, that is oral, and that has been under attack since contact? A school of thought that is still difficult to propose, argue and justify within the academy because it refuses the academy as an ethic, even as the academy cannot reproduce the sort of people who embody this sort of thinking? A kind of theory that is generated through continual practice, that is in constant motion?

As if I was sitting beside him, perhaps visiting with him at the shore of a lake, I listened to Kelley tell Camp that Robinson's work in Black Marxism isn't really about racial capitalism; it is truly about Black revolt. Robinson, he said, traces the source of the ideologies of enslaved Black people to the beliefs, moralities, cosmologies, metaphysics and intellectual traditions of the superstructures they were violently ripped from, not from the modes of production they were forced to labour within. In this I heard ways of thinking, epistemologies, ways of knowing, practices and ethics from Indigenous peoples on the African continent. Kelley traced this influence forward in the Black Radical tradition through the writings of Du Bois, C.L.R. James and Richard Wright—a theory of Black radicalism that developed through what they found in the movements of Black masses.

Listening to this podcast while grooming the trail led me to a moment of revelation. I have for a long time felt an affinity towards the Black feminists and the Black Radical tradition, but also worried that this affinity was a kind of mining for knowledge and practice that I couldn't find in my own community. I stick on the words "couldn't find in my own community" as I write them, because I know with certainty now that this is simply not true. There is an uncompromising, incommensurable critique of colonialism and capitalism from within Nishnaabeg thought, and it not only formed the foundation of resistance for my ancestors, it is the catalyst for my own resistance.

My ancestors, through embodied practice, physical and spiritual, and through our shared "culture"—although I cringe when I type that word because culture cannot stand in for all thought, theory and practice—resisted, critiqued and mobilized against capitalism from the time of contact with Europeans. Our fight is our critique. And as Robinson teaches us, rebellion is an embodied critique that can lead to intellectual traditions—in the case Robinson refers to, the Black Radical tradition. Indigenous peoples mobilized and lived "otherwise" because they had material and ethical imperatives to do so. And this ethical imperative came from the land and the waters, from their intimate relationship to these.

Perhaps this tradition helped produce the kind of thinking that Rebecca Belmore did with water, and the thinking I'm now doing with snow.

My ancestors' critique of capitalism was embodied in a coalition of practices. And it's only in facing the loss of those practices that attempting to write down this critique makes sense.

My ancestors made lives that fit seamlessly into the complicated networks, across scales, that make up the planetary living system. These networks at once fit into the global water cycle, recognize the work of the sun and the moon in the design on the turtle's back, and re-enact the same ethos of networks through interactions with children and family members. From within this frame, capitalism—which presents as greed—must have been immediately recognizable, and appalling, to whoever was on the shoreline when the first "explorers" stepped off the boat in the name of whatever monarchy was demanding empire and loyalty.

My ancestors were very good at sintering, in other words—at living in a way that bonded them to the different forms of life with whom they were sharing time and space. They were building not a Nishnaabeg world, but a Nishnaabeg coalition, working with plant life, animal life and all the other planetary forces that existed before humans. They sintered and wove themselves into the existing fabric of life, working in concert with the planet to renew themselves.

Sintering is fractal-like, expanding and contracting across scales. It is non-linear, iterative, transformative and adaptive. Sintering creates possibility. It is reflected in Indigenous practices of politics, economy and governance. And it is crucial collective work in creating constellations of co-resistance.

5

Gizhiigokwe and Chi'Mikinak

Curve Lake Elder Doug Williams, Gidigaa Migizi, used to tell me that there were at least four origin stories for Nishnaabeg.

There is one where we come from the earth, midwifed into life by the insects, the mnidooshenhag. This took place in the big crack at Kinomagewapkong. There is another story where we spontaneously appear out of thin air. Another where we come from the sky. And one where we come from the water. There are also at least three more migration origin stories—so maybe there are seven origin stories for Nishnaabeg? Then there is the one about the stars and the lily pads . . . or perhaps that fits into the category of sky. And is that category of sky where the Seven-Fires story fits as well? Or is that a separate Gzhwe Manidoo creation story? Maybe the four are leaky containers, carrying water that seeps out, freezes or evaporates, or nurtures a seed that grows into something else.[24]

I think now that Doug's point was that there is a multiplicity of origin stories and a multiplicity of origins.

When I was working with Doug on his book *Michi Saagiig Nishnaabeg: This Is Our Territory*, he insisted that we begin with the Michi Saagiig Nishnaabeg creation story. In the first paragraph he explained why: our original stories, he said, and all the different and unique versions told by our storytellers in different parts of our homeland, "hold our fundamental values and ways of being in the world."[25] He insisted that these stories are our theory, and that our theory is generated through embodied practice across scales. We tell these stories, he told me, because they teach us how to live with each other. And we're supposed to be living the stories.

And then there is his own version of one of the origin stories. Gzhwe Manidoo, Doug began, is a benevolent energy that loves living things unconditionally. Gzhwe Manidoo is at the same time all the genders and none at all.

Loves. As I write those words in this spring moment, in the middle of a miraculous rebirth of leaves and new-growth green, I keep stopping at this point in telling this story that has barely started. I stop because yesterday, a little way along the Jackson Creek trail, I was thinking about the child in me asking who made Gzhwe Manidoo, and how did they exist before the world was created? And on that trail, it occurred to me that this origin story was telling me the answer. It was telling me that the precursor to life, and to world building, wasn't simply a dream or a vision or an intention of something better. It was love. Not a fleeting romantic notion, but a deep sense of care, hope, truth and kindness—a loving any way, and all ways.

Before the idea of the world, before the dreaming, before the making, before the inspiration, the know-how, the inter-communal creations, there was care. There was love.

This story tells us that that love is the necessary precursor to world building.

I understand love encoded in the word *gzhwe* as being unconditional; I understand love as an organizing force, a motion and an ethic of caring. I understand love as communal—not bound up in the individual or with the romantic. And of course, I understand it this way because this is how Doug understood it. As an ethic that is animated within our relations, and from there propels customs of kindness and generates empathy and systems of care for all forms of life that make up our world. It is not a structure that negates emotions or normal responses to the violence of colonialism, responses that might include anger and resentment and even violence. Love in this form is a re-enactment, and like all such practices it can be wholeheartedly manipulated and exploited under colonial rule. It can be conditioned, manipulated and weaponized.

It is also an organizing force in the Nishnaabeg cosmos— one amongst many other organizing forces, but an organizing force nonetheless.

Doug was the Director of Studies for the PhD program in Indigenous Studies at Trent University for many years, and we often co-taught the land-based part of the curriculum. Doug was regularly irritated by the boundaries the university put upon his work, and we often talked about what teaching and learning looks like from within Michi Saagiig Nishnaabeg thought. He thought of education as a microsite of world making. Together we were building a learning community. Together we were making muskrat trappers or sugar makers or ricers. Together we were making food or materials out of the gifts of the land and water.

Doug always began his classes with a calm energy that grounded the students and reinforced community. I would watch how he moved energy through the process of learning, working in concert with the forces around us. He started from a position of unapologetic love of the land, and of the ancestors. He used this love to build a learning community that was spilling over with kindness. In his teaching, there was a complete absence of shaming, authority or criticism. There was, instead, non-interference and trust. There was an expectation of open hearts, hard work and good thoughts. There was no surveillance or agenda. There were very few containers.

When mistakes were made, as they always are, Doug would gently say, "Okay, so what you need to do next is . . ."

The practice of love was the foundation for his regular sugar-bush camps. Doug was this love, and the energy infiltrated the camp. He also reminded us that we should have good thoughts and feelings when we were working with the sap in the forests, and that if we were feeling angry, sad, negative or upset, we should step away, feel our feelings and come back when we were more positive. He explained that our energy and feelings were going into the boiling sap as we spent time with it, and that the syrup would carry that energy. There were also practical considerations for this teaching: sugar making is repetitive, careful work that involves fire and boiling water. When one is upset, it is more difficult to be careful, and that is when accidents happen.

Whether making maple syrup or weaving mats or making baskets, Doug taught us, the energy of the maker is transferred into the belonging, into the creation. This isn't to say that one cannot make things when sad or angry or upset. The Michi Saagiig Nishnaabeg teaching is that these feelings go into the making, and part of our creative sovereignty is to recognize and be responsible for the energy and our intentions.

Doug wrote, "The earth happened, and everything was created instantly and everything was beautiful. This went on for a long time. Everyone was getting along in Nishnaabemowin. We call it kina-bimaadiziwin.

"Everyone was kind."[26]

This is different from mino-bimaadiziwin, the good life or continuous rebirth. *Kina* and *mino* as prefixes are not the same. For global ecosystems to be alive and living mino-bimaadiziwin, and to therefore be continuously regenerating the world, kina-bimaadiziwin must be present. A kindness, but also an imperative that everyone is engaged in this basic premise. There isn't room for racial capitalism in kina-bimaadiziwin.

Some of our origin stories have elaborate explanations for the creation of the world, and sometimes creation is spontaneous and instant. This time, in Doug's story, the world was created instantly, and everything was beautiful.

But, as Doug told us, this peace didn't last. One day, things started to go very wrong. Everything died off, and no one knew why. Doug said, "It could be that life is actually not that easy to keep."

It could be that life is not that easy to keep.

As I write it down, this sentence sticks out in a way it did not when I heard Doug tell the story orally. It sticks out because it is an old Nishnaabeg way of ethically suggesting what happened when one wasn't there as witness. I feel a wave of humility when I read it out loud, and also gratitude. I am reminded that my ancestors did not take life for granted, and the process of keeping each other alive—of keeping oneself alive—was understood, from the beginning, to be dependent upon a profound care for each other and all life.

It could be that life is fragile.

It could be that it took a lot of research and difficult labour to make a sustaining global ecosystem that supported a cacophony of life.

It could be that in making life, we don't always get it right.

It could be that when everything is created instantly and perfectly, it doesn't last.

It could be that life needs continual remaking to renew itself.

It could be that in isolation no individual or community has the knowledge we need to build worlds. It could be that we need to make the knowledge intercommunally.

It could be that world making is struggle.

Doug wrote that although most things died off, the sun, the great waters and the land were saved. Yet all of earthbound life had died and was gone. He said that this *bothered* Gzhwe Manidoo, and that they were upset.

I'm always struck in this passage by Doug's use of the word *bothered*—particularly in a context that involves one so often thought of as Creator or God. *Bothered* encompasses all the feelings of emotional upset—sadness, anger, disappointment, loss, hopelessness and despair. In other words, emotional responses that are healthy for living things experiencing loss and struggle.

This resonates with me now, as I sit on the edge of climate collapse and never-ending world endings.

I imagine Indigiqueer Gzhwe Manidoo in the skyworld, scrolling on their phone, watching Netflix in bed under a weighted blanket, feeling bothered because "the place they had created got into trouble."

But Gzhwe Manidoo doesn't stay in this place for very long. According to Doug, the spirits that lived in the sky went to Gzhwe Manidoo and asked if they could help. The first time Gzhwe Manidoo created the world, they did it alone, and it didn't work. Gzhwe Manidoo was in no state to go back to the earth and start re-creating, so when help was offered, they agreed. They asked another spirit, one who was different in character and work than themselves, for assistance. They asked Gizhiigokwe, Sky Woman, to go down to the earth to see if Creation could be repaired.

The Haudenosaunee have a lot of very beautiful stories about Gizhiigokwe. I mention this as an acknowledgement that our ways of being in the world are different yet intimately linked. We share ecosystems, ecotones, lakes, waterways, politics, ethics, families and many connections. In Doug's story, Gizhiigokwe goes to the earth and finds a partner to try to make life again. It is a collective effort, involving many different spirits, plants and animals. World making, as we see, is necessarily a collective effort of diverse beings. It is a workers' collective.

Gizhiigokwe's work was not easy.

The first time she tried to repair Creation, her two children died. "Something was not working right for Gzhwe Manidoo's dream. It didn't come together," Doug wrote. So Gizhiigokwe went back to the skyworld to visit with Gzhwe Manidoo and try to figure out what happened. I imagine the two felt a deep despair, having both tried and failed. I imagine them both grieving, perhaps stuck in the fog of bereavement and unable to see clearly.

In the meantime, back on earth, a great flood covered the earth with water, washing over and nurturing the land

and changing the physical surface of the earth. Nibi, the water with their own spirit, body of knowledge and autonomy, saw the problem and did the work only they could do, in the hope that this would help move things along.

I find this moment in the story significant, because Nibi didn't have to act. They were fine on their own, existing without the land and landbound life. In fact, given the circumstances of the planet today, I can imagine the oceans being much healthier and sustaining their life without what we know now of our history of land and landbound life. Nibi, though, was thinking beyond themselves and their responsibilities. They were witnessing and listening beyond themselves and towards a new collectivity. Nibi was living in kindness, witnessing and empathizing with the struggle of Gzhwe Manidoo and Gizhiigokwe.

Within Nishnaabeg world making, then, Nibi is crucial. We humans first exist in a water world, a world that meets our needs, and we learn from this what it feels like to be safe. Before our entry into the physical world, Nibi often leads the way, preparing the birth canal for our passage, and then transforming into breast milk to continue their work. Mirroring this process every spring in Nishnaabeg places, Nibi leads the way to growth and renewal, melting from snow to fill creeks and rivers, moving as nutritious sap to prepare trees for new life and providing a catalyst for plant life.

Flooding in the springtime used to be a normal and welcome part of the season, snow transforming to water and replenishing the land with rich minerals and nutrients. Nishnaabeg didn't live on flood plains during the spring so that Nibi could do their work. Along with Nibi's replenishment there was movement and connection, which occurred around the planet: from snow to creek to stream to river to lake to ocean to sky, and then back to the earth. Water that I breathe in becomes a constituent that makes up most of my body. Water that I breathe out becomes part of someone else's body. Water travels the world over, moving easily through land, air, soil, rock and bodies. To say it in another way, Nibi continually violates the home spaces of everything on the planet. It might take a very long time, but Nibi always escapes the container.

Nibi methodically emphasizes that we can build all the enclosures we want, including those of our own bodies, but there are world-making forces, building and maintaining the planet, that are beyond us. In fact, if Nibi is enclosed, they work away, seemingly gently, yet in a manner that is incredibly persistent, and that may leave us unsuspecting until the enclosure is eroded and an undercut or an arch or a hole appears. Nibi never gives up. They keep at it, from the beginning when it seems impossible, through the years of seemingly no progress, to the point where they might be imagining or wishing a transformation, through the hopelessness of incremental change—until finally, after everyone but Nibi has given up, across an incomprehensible time frame for living things, there is a miraculous rupture.

As I think about the work Nibi does, I am reminded that my ancestors didn't struggle with world making the way I'm struggling with it after four centuries of colonialism. My ancestors recognized that worlds existed outside themselves on a planetary scale, composed of an incomprehensible diversity of life, maintained by complex, non-linear cycles. In this sense, they weren't really *world* making, they were building Nishnaabeg lifeways to fit into a much larger communal way of living and bringing forth more life, lifeways that involved every form of creation in every location on the planet. We didn't have to invent anything. We merely had to fit in.

The water, the planet itself, is the blueprint, and its rehearsals each year around the sun create more diversity and more life. Has racial capitalism destroyed the planet and our connection to these forces to the point where we can no longer see, hear and feel the blueprint? Perhaps racial capitalism has destroyed the humility necessary to see that humans are not the conductor of the euphony of life, but instead play the third chair of a bassline instrument?

Perhaps world making isn't up to us, at least not on a planetary scale.

Perhaps world making is communal struggle.

In Doug's story, Gzhwe Manidoo and Gizhiigokwe continued their visit in the skyworld. They comforted each other. Gzhwe Manidoo encouraged Gizhiigokwe and told her not to give up, to keep trying.

> the old ones say
> don't give up
> keep trying
> you'll get it
> maybe
> what you
> need to
> do next
> is don't give up
> keep trying

Nibi's flooding, then, was part of the unseen labour of systems we don't fully understand, working in concert with Gzhwe Manidoo and Gizhiigokwe as they visited, felt, rested and then tried again. I am reminded of Kanaka Maoli scholar Noelani Goodyear-Ka'ōpua's writing about hulihia as an overturning, a catastrophic upheaval followed by churning that eventually slows—and as a result, our lives are permanently altered or transformed.[27]

In Doug's telling, after spending time in the skyworld, Gizhiigokwe made the decision to go back to earth and keep trying. She encounters Nibi's flood—the catastrophic upheaval that left the world in a completely different place from when she was last there. I imagine Gizhiigokwe struggling to find a place to begin. While the skyworld is her homeplace, the earth had been a place she could visit. But now, Nibi's work gives her an endless expanse of water, her usual beginning places drowned. It must have been difficult to return, remembering the loss of her two children and seeing Gzhwe Manidoo's grief over the catastrophic loss of life from their first world.

I think now about Gizhiigokwe and Gzhwe Manidoo, and all the plants, animals and humans in diaspora, and all those who have never ever known their homelands. I think alongside the ones who witness daily a catastrophic loss of life on the planet, the ones who see the arithmetic that places Black life as disposable and Indigenous life as extractable. The ones who don't know where to begin, or how to do what they must, but come together to do the work anyway.

Here is the world. It's only water. There is no land. There is no land-back because there are no homelands. There are no territories. There are no humans.

Gizhiigokwe is still here. Gzhwe Manidoo is still here. Nibi is still here. The sun and the moon are still here.

There's still a lot of life here.

There are still a lot of stories here.

Kinetic and potential are still here.

The world is still.

Still love.

And so I return to Doug's story. In time, Gizhiigokwe found animals in the water that had survived the flood because they could swim—turtles, beavers and muskrats. Chi'Mikinak (Snapping Turtle) came to the surface and offered Gizhiigokwe a place to land and rest. The animals Gizhiigokwe found needed help. They needed care. They needed a place to rest because they had been swimming endlessly for days. Gizhiigokwe saw the need, as did the snapping turtle and the animals that could live both on land and in water. Maybe they weren't thinking of making a world at this point. Maybe they were thinking only of caring for the ones that were near exhaustion. Maybe they worked together to meet the material needs of their immediate community, which meant making a place to rest. A homeplace. A space where care work could take place to regenerate bodies and souls struggling in the sea.

Each being gave up what they could in support of others:

a homespace on their back
a homespace in the homespace of another
with not a speck of earth in sight

Gizhiigokwe rested on the back of the turtle Chi'Mikinak, alongside beavers, turtles and muskrats. It was a communal place of refuge. A community. A homespace.

Over time, Gizhiigokwe noticed the design on Chi'Mikinak's back. She ran her finger around the rim of the shell and felt its meaning:[28] 13 parts in the middle, 28 parts around the edge. She felt its meaning because her body cycled each moon, and her body's practice of cycles enabled her to see the moon's cycles on the turtle's back. She felt her life experience in what she saw.

Kanaka Maoli
already
know
this
love
is the practice
of an awakened mind
ulu a'e ke welina a ke aloha[29]

Gizhiigokwe thought the turtle was carrying something special.

a thought
a recipe
a code
a hint
a fragment
a suggestion
a mapping

Chi'Mikinak didn't instruct or speak or even tell a story. Like Nibi, Chi'Mikinak saw Gizhiigokwe's struggle and offered a place to rest. That is all. It was up to Gizhiigokwe to stay calm and curious and hopeful. It was up to Gizhiigokwe to connect the map that Chi'Mikinak had shared with her to another creation story, the one where the world wasn't created instantly. The story where Gzhwe Manidoo laboured, creating circles upon circles through Seven Fires. The one with potential and kinetics. The one where the movement was circular. It was up to Gizhiigokwe to find the meaning in the design.

love
thought | feeling
light | spectrum
potential | kinetics
network | renewal
tears | thanksgiving
everything

Gizhiigokwe recognized the turtle's map because they knew cycles. They knew cycles because their body cycled. Lots of bodies cycle, and all genders can cycle, and many do not. The cycle Gizhiigokwe saw and recognized was the one with the number 28 and the number 13.

And Gizhiigokwe understood that Chi'Mikinak was showing her what was missing in Gzhwe Manidoo's previous design: cycling and renewal. Not even Gzhwe Manidoo is perfect, because the job of Gzhwe Manidoo isn't perfection; the job of Gzhwe Manidoo is unconditional love.

Chi'Mikinak's shell was a map of cycles: 13 moons, 28 days each. Turtles still carry that map today, and so do people who menstruate. It was a cycle of renewal that brought forth more life—cyclical movement embodied across scales, from inside bodies to ocean tides to the phases of the moon.

I like that perfection isn't an ingredient in world making. In Nishnaabeg origin stories, there are always mistakes and missteps, and those mistakes and missteps can lead to more learning, stronger relationships and resilience.

Gzhwe Manidoo (God!?) didn't have the knowledge they needed to build the universe. They had to work with others to generate the knowledge they collectively needed to build the world.

the space
in between
interstitial
interspatial
intervening
space
intercommunal

From this story I understand that we must generate the knowledge we need to form new worlds. And I understand that there are many kinds of knowledge and many sites of knowledge generation.

In Doug's telling, once Gizhiigokwe was settled on Chi'Mikinak's back, and once they'd visited, floated, rested, breathed, they were joined by water animals, the ones from the land that were undrowned from the flood. And they made room, and all rested together.

Chi'Mikinak floated in perfect balance with their shell at the surface, carrying more and more weight as the resting land and sky animals joined Gizhiigokwe. But it was difficult to maintain equilibrium as more and more weight was added, and this generated the idea within Chi'Mikinak that they needed soil to make the world again.

Gizhiigokwe was sitting on Chi'Mikinak's back and all the water animals were floating and watching. Loon, a bird that could swim as well as float, offered to dive to the bottom of the water. The Loon was gone for a long time, and finally floated to the surface, drowned. As Doug told it, "The loon had tried so hard, it died trying."[30] The same thing happened with the Otter. And then the same with the Beaver.

World making, in this telling, involves individual and collective sacrifice.

Next came Muskrat, and the same thing happened. Muskrat tried too hard and floated to the surface, drowned. But when they floated to the surface, Gizhiigokwe noticed they had a handful of earth. She put the handful of dirt onto Chi'Mikinak's back, and it grew into mountains, streams, lakes, and then into clouds, winds, rain, trees and beautiful animals.

Sometimes, in plowing through, there is a larger benefit to others.

When this happened, Gizhiigokwe stepped back, just as Gzhwe Manidoo had done before. Now the planet could replenish itself through cycles, and so long as things remained in balance, it would reproduce life in perpetuity. Gizhiigokwe, like Gzhwe Manidoo, was no longer the Creator. She had completed her work and now the responsibility for bringing forth new life rested collaboratively with all living things that make up the planet.

Gizhiigokwe went back to the skyworld, Doug told us, where she became the moon. She became the one to watch over and regulate the cycles needed to bring forth more life on earth. She embodied the knowledge and responsibility she had understood in the design on Chi'Mikinak's back, which was key to producing more life. She lives there still, watching over women and children and queer people—and in my mind, everyone who sees themselves in her story. She is there for unconditional love and advice and care work, working in partnership with the sun to provide light in the darkness. As her form cycles, she reflects through her phases the cyclical nature of the universe. Her presence brings to mind the intertwined and interdependent circles, cycles and pathways of reciprocity across time and space, all of which take the fragility of life and make it sustainable.

Meanwhile, Gizhiigokwe took on different names so that everyone could relate: the name is Nokomis to some, Dibik-Giizis to others and Gizhiigokwe to still others. From this I understand that names aren't enclosures; they are the expansive story making of the universe.

World making requires love, kindness and care. It requires collectivity and relationality, and it is these practices that generate the knowledge needed to move on to the next step. Through his stories, Doug reinforced this for me, and for many others. He told us that there are many kinds of knowledge and many sites of knowledge production. There are many origins. The land and the waters, the universe, hold all the knowledge we need to make other worlds.

World building is difficult global work. It is sacrifice, both collective and individual. It requires difference and diversity.

There is no centre or centring in the creation and maintenance of a network.

Mappings of the Liminal

I think about being in the bush with Doug—how I was often in my head, not paying attention to my surroundings and the bits of knowledge the land was sharing with me. But each March, as we collected sap from the maple trees, Doug would describe the melting of the snow, the warmth of the sun at midday and the crispness of the nighttime. He would turn my attention to the waking of the trees, the making of sap within their trunks, their regrowth and their breath. He talked about Ziigwan as a season that would hand things over to Minookmi, the second part of spring when the broad leaves are born and the tree frogs begin to sing—spirits bringing with them a miraculous transformation that he found wonderful every year.

A miraculous transformation that happens every year.

Now, hearing Doug's voice in this time of world endings and world beginnings grounds my thinking in a different register. Over the past twenty years the acceleration of the global climate crisis has not brought about any transformation where global systems have aligned with the existing planetary cycles that create and maintain life on earth. Rather, there has been an intensification of racial capitalism and its hierarchies, violences that see Black, Brown and Indigenous peoples as sacrificial in order to maintain the wealth of a few elite, wealthy white men. Over the course of my own life, this has become much worse—and the speed at which things are becoming worse is also accelerating.

I am reminded that my ancestors are here with me, supporting and sharing and caring for me from another realm. They are present in Gzhwe Manidoo, and they allow me to be present within an unconditional love for the living beings that make up our planetary homespace. The energy of Gzhwe Manidoo lands in my heart, singing to me that the violence of colonialism requires an arsenal of coping mechanisms, and the full range of emotions—including anger, resentment, sadness, despair and hopelessness—are necessary responses and motivators alongside a foundational habit of care and kindness and unconditional love. These ethics are foundational in that they create worlds that view private property, prisons, punishment and greed as terrible mistakes. Gzhwe Manidoo grounds me in my body as a cycle of energies through space and time, and in the notion that the individual exists only fleetingly and insignificantly.

I know, too, that the experiences of Gzhwe Manidoo and Gizhiigokwe eliminate the possibility that this work will be easy and spontaneous. Their stories tell us that there was no map. There was no research plan. There was no set of strategies. There was no land. There was no leader— or there were many leaders.

There was, however, a practice of love and hope. There was a fostering of emergence. There was a collaborative practice of kindness. There was persistence, and perhaps the belief that eventually, working together, these beings would generate what they collectively needed to get to the next day. They understood that in remaking the world, they weren't building an entire planetary system but merely figuring out how to live within, and contribute to, the cycles that already existed and had given them life.

There are many origin stories that tell of this kind of knowledge.

Joshua Myers begins his book *Cedric Robinson: The Time of the Black Radical Tradition* with a description of the philosophies and ethical practices for world making of the Bakongo peoples of West-Central Africa. Using the work of Congolese intellectual Tata Kimbwandende Kia Bunseki Fu-Kiau, Myers grounds the evolving world view and theory of a particular communal existence that is both cyclical and deeply relational.[31] He describes a world that is at once concerned with the intimate and the planetary, and an existence where to be alive is "to seek to understand, grow, and mature in rhythm with ancestors and the natural world, and to align them with a vision of and for community" within the tuzingu—the records of their ancestors and the bodies of knowledge they housed and embedded into the intellectual practices of the Bakongo. Myers then uses these understandings as a conceptual foundation for one definition of the Black Radical tradition found in the work of Cedric Robinson.

Robinson himself, as Myers notes, described the Black Radical tradition in Black Marxism as "an accretion (process of growth), over generations, of collective intelligence gathered from struggle," and as "enslavement providing the occasion for struggle" wherein connection, record-keeping and creating a collective body of intelligence—all with the purpose of bringing forth more life—were consistent with the theories of the Bakongo peoples.

I'm drawn to this section of Myers's book, and I read and reread it. First, because the theories of the Bakongo peoples are so like the theories of my own people, the Nishnaabeg. And second, because of the continuation of this orientation and accretion within the political movements of radical and liberatory Black organizing. The second point is most striking to me. If I were to sit down and try to excavate an Indigenous liberatory or radical politics, I would most certainly find evidence of it at every point in history since the beginning of colonialism, and I would have to increasingly disentangle this from the recognition politics of the state. And yet, as Tata Kimbwandende Kia Bunseki Fu-Kiau points out, coding and decoding, tying and untying, are critical parts of world-making practices.[32]

Lakota philosopher Vine Deloria Jr., in *God Is Red*, writes that one of the most significant differences between Indigenous and Western metaphysics is that land is central to Indigenous modes of thinking and being and to our ethical formulations. He writes that places or place making are sites of meaning making, "the highest possible meaning," and that most Western societies, by contrast, derive meaning from time in relation to place, with the narrative of development and history being of central importance. Deloria concludes that this fundamental difference, with Indigenous peoples philosophically concerned with space and Western peoples philosophically concerned with time, makes understanding and meaning between the two thought systems difficult.

I remember when I first bought *God Is Red*. I was visiting Boulder, Colorado, in the late 1990s and I found the

book in a local bookstore. I was a hungry PhD student at
the University of Manitoba, and this was a time when if one
found a book by a Native writer, one bought it. Revisiting
the book decades later, after spending years immersed in
Michi Saagiig Nishnaabewin, shifts my understanding.

Following Deloria, I don't think I understand a clear
division between time and space; rather, I understand time
as a function of the networks created by space. The passage
of time within Nishnaabeg thought is not linear, and it
comes from the cycles of living and non-living systems that
make up the land. Time is inferred from place.

A day is one rotation of the earth on its axis, or two passages of the sun across the meridian. Using stars, a day is the
period of two passages of a star across the earth's meridian.
A month is the time needed to complete the cycle phases of
the moon, or the moon's passage around the earth. A year
is the period taken by the earth to complete an orbit around
the sun. Time is movement. Time places the earth and all the
patterns and systems that make up the earth in liminal space.

I'm thinking about this in Denendeh in June, where
the sun is seemingly always out, high in the sky. Darkness
comes for a few hours after midnight, more muted daylight than actual darkness. This contrasts with the dark of
December and January, when the sun only appears for a
few hours each day. These seasonal contrasts in daylight are
an organizing feature of life in the north, and the farther
one goes, the more dramatic the contrast is, until you reach
Inuit homelands where there are long periods of dark in the
winter and long periods of midnight sun in the summer. In
this period of expanded daylight, event after event can occur
as life continues long into what was previously understood

as night. Plants grow at phenomenal rates. Animals adjust their circadian rhythms to the ever-changing levels of light, with birds seemingly singing at all hours. While this measurement is non-spatial, it is informed by place, space or land. It is informed by days, months and seasons. And these, in turn, are informed by the movement of the sun, the rotation of the earth, one's location on the planet. Cyclical time comes from land. Linear time is a European construct that overlays cyclical time—a mechanism to organize the world in a homogeneous way to facilitate, of course, capitalism.

When my kids were little, I tried each December to recover some of the celebrations and traditions of my Michi Saagiig Nishnaabeg ancestors, so as to bring authentic meaning to the month. The winter solstice seemed to make sense. For a few years we gathered around an outside fire and told stories to mark the day. This wasn't how my ancestors would have marked the occasion. Doug had shared with me that they would send a child out with a device that measured the movements of the sun at noon. The device was sinew or string and a stick, now commonly known as a shadow stick. Or often the stick was a tree. Children would draw a circle on the ground and place the stick in the circle. A week or two before the solstice, they would mark the length of the shadow at noon, relative to the circle. They would repeat this process each day. At some point the shadow would stop lengthening and begin to shorten—and that was the winter solstice.

Doug told me that our name for winter solstice is *Shkwaamaagee Giizis*—meaning "no more movement" or "the end of movement" or "the sun is now standing still," where *giizis* meant moon or month. After it stops for about three weeks—Nike zhaw miinawaa—it comes back.

We would mark this time of year, Gchi Gisinaa Giizis, by feasting, having ceremony and celebrating on the first full moon after December 21.[33]

Time is a mapping of cycles. A mapping of liminal space.

I think of a child in the time before colonization, in the darkness of December, measuring light on the snow with a stick and sinew, connecting themselves and their family to planetary movements and cycles as a practice. I think of other ways this happens for Michi Saagiig Nishnaabeg, which of course includes sunrise, noon, sunset, midnight, which are sometimes thought of as the four sacred times of day. Sunrise and our sunrise ceremonies are the first daily reminder that we are attached to something communal and global that is far bigger than any one of us. The light before dawn helps us visualize that the presence is a collapse, an enfolding, of the past and the future. Naawakwe, or noon, is another stopping time, with the sun high in the sky during the summer. Sunset is yet another transformation—a handing over from Giizis to Dibi-Giizis. And midnight is the fourth stopping point. The thirteen moons that make up the year are signals telling us that the impossible blue of the planet is liminal space. Everything is always in transition.

From within this frame, spatial orientation is relational rather than a fixed territory. From inside this orientation, linear time is a ruse. With this orientation, a division between time and space is an artifact of a way of thinking that is a fantasy.

All the water that surrounded that child in the time before colonization, in the darkness of December, every single drop, is all the water that has ever been on the planet— and is all the water that now surrounds me.

Water is the network that facilitates communication and relationship between all forms of life.

Water is a liminal space, always shifting between states.

This network, Water, Nibi, is the container of life on our planet, and as a container it is constantly moving and changing form, taking up different amounts of space. It is an anti-container container.

Three percent of it, fresh water, moves inside and outside all forms of life. It exists in soil and air.

Without cycling, process and a complicated positive feedback loop, without Gizhiigokwe's invention and monitoring of the cycles, there is no container. Gizhiigokwe, Sky Woman, created liminal space and transformation.

Fresh water accounts for less than 3 percent of water on the planet.

Of that less than 3 percent, two-thirds is frozen in glaciers and ice caps. The other 30 percent is groundwater. Only 0.3 percent of fresh water is found in lakes, rivers and swamps.[34]

The earth is 70 percent water.

The human body is 60 percent water. Animals are 60 to 80 percent water. Plants are 90 percent water.

The liminal space of water is a complex cycle spanning different scales of time—spending just days in the atmosphere and decades in snow and glaciers, and thousands of years in the ocean, and tens of thousands of years underground, and hundreds of thousands of years in the Antarctic ice shelf.[35]

A drop of water inside me appears on my skin as sweat in the summer. This evaporates into the air, travelling as water vapour. Its travels expose it to conditions that cause it to undergo condensation, and it falls to the earth as some kind of precipitation. It can fall and be collected in the

ocean. It can fall into the collection of groundwater, inter-
cepted by soil, infiltration and percolation, learning to move
sideways. It can run off into a lake or a river that moves it to
the ocean. It can be transpired, perspired, expired by plants
and animals.

And still, it is in motion. And still, it is all the water in
the world today. Every drop is all the water that has ever
been on the planet.

And all life shares this water.

Un-mappings Leading
to Everywhere and Nowhere

In November 2021, Dionne Brand's book *A Map to the Door of No Return* was miraculously enacted as ceremony, a gathering site, a travelling place, a celebration, and of course as a mapping and an unmapping, by a brilliant formation of artists and writers thinking alongside and practising waywardness.[36] The gathering took place virtually, and therefore allowed people from all over the world to witness, participate and present. It was unlike any gathering I've ever experienced, for a few reasons. It was unapologetically intellectual. Thinkers, writers and artists brought excellence; no one winged it or wrote their paper the night before. Respect for the work was embodied in the calibre of the responses to it. There was nothing superficial or performative. There was nothing without equal measures of heart.

I was invited to contribute a short reflection on this twentieth anniversary of the book's publication. I re-found my copy on the endless and chaotic bookshelves in my house and began reading it during a time when the urban and online Indigenous communities were embroiled in, and justly irritated by, what has become known as the Pretend-

ian scandal—or a scandal around belonging, and the enclosures around citizenship and membership in our nations.
I shut down the fearful voices in my head and read the
book with my heart only.

I listened and I felt.

And in particular, I read and reread the chapter titled
"Pinery Road and Concession 11."

I calculated temporally when Brand might have been
living in *my territory* outside Kinmount, Ontario, in a cabin
in the woods. I thought about what I had been doing in that
same period.

I thought about how my ancestors would never have
said "my territory," and wondered about the trajectory that
enabled those two words to slip so effortlessly and perhaps
thoughtlessly from my lips.

And then, instead of writing, I got in my car and drove
to Pinery Road and Concession 11. I took as my companion
a Black Ash Basket—a basket that had found its way to me
through a series of family and friends. I was returning it to
the cultural centre at Curve Lake First Nation, which is on the
way to Pinery Road.

In the car with *Map* on the dashboard and the basket in
the back seat, I thought about place, belonging, diaspora,
property, plantation and foreclosure.

When I reached the corner where Brand's car had broken
down in the winter twenty years prior, I could feel the white
gaze watching me from behind curtains and fences, on lawns
and between chores. I could hear the warning barks of dogs.
I could see the intersecting worlds—dirt roads, farms, quad
trails, produce stands amongst fragments of bush. My body
filled with anxiety, rage, standoffishness and humiliation.

Taking all this in, I had the idea of leaving a surveillance camera at the corner over a twenty-four-hour period to take time-lapse photographs. I enlisted my partner, an artist and maker, to make a device with our collection of old iPhones, duct tape and battery packs. We decided to time-lapse-record the journey there and back too, in case the device failed, and I ended up liking the mapping of movement and travel.

The surveillance device worked well enough, although not for the full twenty-four hours. It caught settlers moving around, attending Thanksgiving dinners, quadding through the bush; it caught dogs, police and the mundane goings-on of whiteness.

And it caught a glimpse of what it feels like to be Nishnaabeg near the Burnt River, outside Kinmount, Ontario. This was a different situation and feeling from what Brand describes—but one related by history and oppression and erasure nonetheless.

MAPPING AND UNMAPPING

When Sky Woman, Gizhiigokwe, came to the ocean world a second time to try to make a new world, she found a kind of map on the back of the turtle. It wasn't a map that documented property or borders or topography. It didn't show a route. It wasn't even instructional. It was a map that made visible the nature of time itself. It showed 13 full moons in the 13 sections that make up the core of the shell. It showed the 28 phases of each moon around the edge of the shell as an influential organizing force. It made visible movement and transformation and flux. And it made visible the work of the night sun—work that went beyond lighting the night sky. The map was presented as resting place, as a material answer, for those who were undrowned, to the problem of finding such a place in oceans of water.[37] Because of the map, Gizhiigokwe stopped searching for the route to the new world and looked inside herself to make a crucial connection: the insight that the missing essence in Gzhwe Manidoo's initial attempt at world making was cycling and spiralling and returning again and again. The missing essence was renewal and reciprocity. The turtle's shell was a map to nowhere—and a map to the whole world.

The map on the snapping turtle's back is not a two-dimensional drawing of the assets of colonial thought and life; it is not a grid on white paper or white screens tracing a route through history and development from the savage to the civilized.

The turtle-shell map is like the sunrise. It is visual mapping of the collapsing past and future, giving birth to the present.

It is a reminder.

If I were to make a map of *my territory*, it would be a song. Song begins inside me. It is a kind of wrestling to articulate the incompleteness of what is inside me, using my poor understanding of my body as instrument, and breathing to fuel that instrument. The sound would originate in me and travel. There would be seen and unseen parts. It would be a fleeting record of a series of relationships in the cycling of time.

It would lead nowhere and everywhere.

If I were to draw a map of *my territory*, it would be a series of fine un-linear lines moving in every direction on the page and into the page, through the page and around the page. There would be so many lines my map would look like a single homogeneous colour of whatever ink I started with. The density would grow with each trip I make around the sun, until the paper gives way, ruptures, and I am left still drawing.

If I were to draw a map of *my territory*, I would have to start at the beginning with the sound of corn in a turtle rattle and my heartbeat.

If I were to draw a map of *my territory*, I would have to start inside the otolith of a salmon from the lake, and then with the mucus of an eel newly arrived with news of the Sargasso Sea. I would add the migration route across the lake for the birds on their way south and then north. I would add the migration route inside the lake for the fish.

If I were to draw a map of *my territory*, the page would be blank with all the life and lives and living that go into the making of paper from trees and water and sunlight, all the lives and living that go into my existence that I don't know.[38]

This morning, at the end of this world, I ask myself what I would give up to bring into being a different world, to change the air, to change everything.[39] I theoretically sort through precious things to see which ideas are brick walls and which are doorways. I think of the snapping turtle's shell design, and I think about all the maps I'm missing, even though they are right in front of me. The maps all around us. The ones on the backs of turtles.

Pinery Road and Concession 11

The sky is dressed in seven shades of grey, and I am dressed in seven shades of sky.[40]

The basket is in the back seat, loosely wrapped in an opaque plastic garbage bag, waiting for its ride home. It's different from other baskets I've seen in my life. It is a darker colour. It's also bigger, with fancier detailing. I think it's made of the black ash, baapaagigun, that we can barely find around here nowadays. The old ones used to harvest a tree, canoe it back to the reserve and then pound the log until the annual rings would separate into splints. The splints were woven into baskets. I imagine the fancier ones were sold to white folks and the mediocre ones were kept around our tents and shacks and cabins to hold our belongings.

What I see is that this basket is a body made from the years of baapaagigun's life. Each of those annual rings recorded growth and weather. Each one of those orbits was a document of light, heat, water and nourishment. I think of who might have harvested the tree and paddled it back to the community. I think of who might have done the pounding to make the splints. I think of the women who wove those years into something else. I think of the woman who paddled her canoe on Chemong, going from cottage to cottage, selling and trading her hours for clothes and food for her family.

We leave the city, driving through farmland speckled with election signs for Conservative and People's Party of Canada candidates. When we turn onto the reserve and cross the border, every telephone pole is wrapped in red cloth. I tell Baapaagigun-makak this is because one of their young women was recently murdered by her white boyfriend.

The one that loved catching frogs.[42]

We pass wooden cut-outs of children dressed in pure love, carrying the words "every child matters." I tell Baapaagigun-makak that we're allowed to be furious and sad now, within reason.

The one that ran away from school and into the bush,
followed Jimkoons and Madden around—
the ones that didn't bring lunch to the bush
instead eating seagull and loon eggs,
water snakes and frogs,
porcupines and squirrels,
muskrats and turtles.[43]

I wonder if Baapaagigun-makak is looking out the car window for their relatives. Those relatives will be hard to find. Much of the black ash was cleared by colonizers for farming and settlement, and the remaining trees are under threat from the emerald ash borer, an invasive beetle that came to North America inside packaging and wooden crates.

We stop at the old man's house beside the dump, but he isn't home. I use his outhouse and am overjoyed when

I find an empty peanut butter jar with half a roll of toilet paper inside. Back on the road, we pass a lonely orange election sign as we pull into the cultural centre. The curator meets us, and through our pandemic-era face masks we talk. I retell the story of the eighty or so years Baapaagigunmakak travelled from a Nishnaabeg woman in a canoe on the shoreline, to a white lady's cottage on Chemong Lake, to a house in my birthplace, to my parents' house, and then to my sister's house in Toronto, and finally to my house in Nogojiwanong. And then here.

In a quiet voice, he says, "Welcome home."

"We'll show the basket to Doug," he says. "We'll show the basket to the Elders Advisory Circle. They might be able to tell who it belongs to by the signature in the style. Miigwech for bringing this home."

I stop for cheap gas,
a paper map,
bad coffee.

There are no paper maps.

It's September—the second September of the pandemic. We've now been charged with the task of "living with the virus," which is code for the arithmetic that allows some of us to live without carrying the burden of those who succumb. A code for the calculation of who we will sacrifice to line the pockets of those with the money.[44]

The air is heavy with grief. There is a change in the light as the first cool air marks the time of year when our kids were stolen; and when they still take our kids, to remake them into people with pockets lined with money. Summer may have held space for running and laughing and shrieking around, but there is no space for that in the fall. There is no space for the sounds of children.

After I leave the reserve, instead of going back to the city, I head in the opposite direction, past Miskwaa Ziibi, which used to be called Squaw River. In 1993, some of the Elders at Curve Lake First Nation, led by Gladys Taylor, launched a complaint to the Ontario Geographic Names Board to have the name of Squaw River changed back to its original name, Miskwaa Ziibi, meaning Red River. I think this will be the only time today I see my language.

Next, I pass Nogie's Creek. It is littered with ice cream shops and paddleboard rental shacks, campers and cottages. None of these people will know that Chief Nogie led Curve Lake First Nation from 1830 to 1848. He was exiled from the reserve to this place by the Indian agent and the missionaries. This was no real hardship for him—Nogie's Creek was a beautiful place where he and his family could live a good life away from the surveillance of Indian agents and God.[45]

I squint to see the good life.

As I turn onto Burnt River Road, I inhabit a familiar sense of dread. Oh yes, this is Michi Saagiig Nishnaabeg land, and I am grateful to be in a car that is working well, with doors that lock. I am grateful to have a cellphone. I pass more signs to elect Conservative and People's Party of Canada candidates. I pass the sign for the Somerville Tract, land that was purchased by the County of Victoria in 1928. The land was cleared for agricultural use by settlers then abandoned when it wasn't fertile enough. Red, white and

Scotch pines were planted. The plantation is managed by the Ministry of Natural Resources.

The trees are planted close together, in rows, like corn. They are the wrong species for this place. They form a forest that doesn't have any parents or language because there is only one kind of tree, and they are all the exact same age. There were only children, and they grew up as best they could.

I sit in the plantation's width.[46]

Nishnaabeg carried travel routes in their heads, routes that were passed down and had an east-west orientation rather than a north-south one, focused on creeks, streams, rivers, lakes and portages. These maps were stories upon stories of each time people had travelled the route, and of each time their parents and grandparents had travelled those same rivers and lakes. They were stories of storms and hard times. Of meet-ups and good luck. The bends and riffles, mnemonic devices for memories. The smells and sounds, reminders of the route. Each journey, another ring.

To travel, one had to float and paddle, with rivers and lakes doing the carrying. Every destination was temporary. Home, always temporary. Home, always shared.

Home, always a shared practice.

Homelessness, always a shared practice.[47]

akii-mazina'igan

akii meaning the earth, the land

mazina'igan a book, a letter, a document, a paper[48]

A book, a letter, a document, a paper. When the colonizers came, they were always lost because they refused to live in the network of the living. The colonizers needed a book, a letter, a document, a compass, a paper, a policy, a law, an accounting, so that they could build fences and put up signs that said No Trespassing and Private Property.

I am getting close to why I came. Dread fills my stomach with sharpness. My dread, of course, is not in the same register as Brand's when she writes "This place fills me with a sense of dread, but also a sense of mystery."[49] Our histories and diasporas are different. What brought her to this place and now brings me, decades later, are different yet entwined.

My dread is commingled with shame. I should feel comfortable here. I should feel connected, as if I belong. I should be stronger than my fear of these landowners. I should insert myself where I don't see myself. I should know the name of Burnt River in my language. I should want to live here in a cabin and write books and do ceremony and tap maple trees.

I should, and I don't.

Sometimes the land defeats you, just the sum of it.[50]

I am old enough to know that coming here, this retracing, will not likely lead to finding whatever it is I'm looking for.

I am old enough to know that when I reach Pinery Road and Concession 11, there won't be much of anything.

I am old enough to know that I won't find home. But I might feel—we might all feel—a little less alone.

9

"Where My Mother Held Me"

"I don't know if there is a child
   Anywhere on this earth, that
   Wasn't at least once, held
   By their mother. Water: where
   My mother held me until I was
   Given to land."[51]

Over the course of his life, Doug taught hundreds of people like me. He understood well that, for our people, the overlap between generations is a fertile site for knowledge, and our system relies on this overlap to ensure that our most precious knowledge makes it through to the next generation. Doug passed away in July 2022. Now that Doug is gone, I rely on one of his other students, Maddy Whetung, in order to hear his voice and access his wisdom. I'm eternally grateful to Maddy because, although we are of the same culture and are both academics and parents who spent a lot of time on the land with Doug,[52] we're also very different people, at different life stages, and we learned different things from him. As I wade through grief, I'm grateful to hear Doug through Maddy; and I'm particularly grateful to hear his knowledge, through her, on the shore.

Maddy's family is from Curve Lake, and because she is younger than me, she didn't get to spend the same amount of time with Doug. Maddy's pandemic research journey was complex. Between stay-at-home orders and sickness, Maddy was pregnant, gave birth and became a mother. And during this same period, Doug died. Through all of it, the two of us would go for walks on the shore of Jackson Creek, talking about her dissertation work and my theory of water.

Mohawk midwife Katsi Cook teaches that another person is our first environment, because we all begin life in water in the womb.[53] Our origins are in water, in pregnant bodies, being carried and growing life for nine months in amniotic fluid—the same water that is in the lake whose shores I walk, sometimes with Maddy and sometimes alone.

Now, sitting at the shore, I'm thinking of my own relationship to water in this way—as my first environment inside my mom, my first world. It's a world I can't remember, but one that is my origin nonetheless—a world in which I was encased, a shoreline of sorts, an overlapping of bodies and spirits. And I'm thinking that this start in life, in a womb filled with water, gives me a responsibility to remember, to speak out, to speak about waterways and shorelines. I'm remembering, too, the time when I was pregnant, and new life was growing inside me—when I was on the other side of that shore, breathing for another, breathing for the future, until the new life could breathe on its own, as M. NourbeSe Philip writes.[54] The borders and boundaries of pregnant bodies change from a single body into two enmeshed bodies, two separating bodies, and finally, after the umbilical cord has been cut, two separate but linked bodies. There is constant yet changing and intimate communication between the two beings about each other's needs—one living in the world of water, one living in air and on land.

This is the original relationship from which humans begin. All humans.

Elders and medicine people talk about birth as a ceremony, and as a doorway between the spiritual world and the physical world. In our tradition, ceremonies can often be a doorway to another world or another sort of consciousness. For instance, a doorway is opened when a spirit is lowered from the skyworld, through a pregnancy, to the earth. Ceremonies such as a shaking tent, fasting or Sweat Lodges can open doorways to speak to spirits and ancestors in the spirit world. Sacred fires can also be doorways to the spirit world, which is why we place offerings in the flames. Through these ceremonies, Elders and medicine people make ways for us to visit with our ancestors and the spirit world. And these doorways connect us to forces and realities that we don't fully understand but which are part of our network nonetheless. Participants in these ceremonies are taught not to talk about what happens inside the lodges, in part to provide a confidential space for other participants, and in part, I think, because our spiritual lives and systems have been under attack from the Church and the State for so many decades. I will say that these spaces where spirits of eagles—or spirits of grandparents, or beings that exist only in the spirit world—enter and relate to individual participants gave me a profound sense of humility and a realization that the physical world I know through experience and Elders and science is only part of the picture.

Still, doorways or spaces in between are not world building in and of themselves. We go through the portal, but the natural world is still there in front of us. The foundation of the new world is still there—an interdependent network of living beings that lives and reproduces itself. In a sense, the network is the map. It is the instructions. And humans have a very incomplete, impoverished understanding of how we fit into this network and how the network works. All "species" have this incomplete map because we each are only one piece of the puzzle. We need to commune with each other to put the puzzle together. We need to commune to understand the instructions, and to keep the network balanced, functioning and bringing forth more life. We need to commune to build our worlds that fit within the natural world in a way that brings forth more life. The natural world is made up of many worlds, many stories, many portals.

Maddy's work on the shore asks me to be present at the shore. Before, when I was at the shore, I was going elsewhere and was focused on getting things into the canoe, or getting things out of the canoe, getting water, chopping wood, maintaining the map. Coming to understand Maddy's academic work on gender, shoreline law and Nishnaabeg relational policies along the Trent-Severn Waterway changed that for me. She begins her paper with the point at which, in 1833, colonialism captured Nibi and our network, when "six white-settler men conspired to build a canal system of locks and dams connecting Lake Ontario to Georgian Bay. These men were powerful, upper-class settlers who conceived of this waterway as a public enterprise toward their own material gain . . . they argued it would increase settlement and bring capitalism to the area."[55]

Bring capitalism to the area.

Capitalism had already brought Champlain, and a host of other invaders, into our home in search of capital in the form of white pine and timber, beaver pelts, minerals and farmland. By 1833 in Kina Gchi Nishnaabeg ogamig, the place where we all live and work together, my ancestors were acutely aware that white people were not interested in sharing, a rubric of care or the welfare of any living thing other than themselves. I imagine this selfishness would have been shocking and laughable, in the same way it still is today.

The Burnt River flows into Cameron Lake. Cameron Lake is between Lock 34 and Lock 35 on the Trent-Severn Waterway, and this is the map to why, standing on the corner of Pinery Road and Concession 11, I felt lonely, in spite of clutching the *Map to the Door of No Return* and thinking alongside Dionne Brand.

According to ecologists, Kina Gchi Nishnaabeg ogamig— or ogaming—is an ecotone, meaning it is a transitional zone between two ecosystems, the Canadian Shield, with its boreal forests and rocky outcroppings, and the Great Lakes–St. Lawrence Lowlands, with its hardwood forests and black oak savannas. The two ecotones overlap, creating an explosion of biological diversity. Scientists like to use ecological bracketing[56] as a way to impose enclosure, sameness and borders around ecosystems, a way of making complex open systems simpler and closed so as to have enough control to study them. I'm sure my ancestors would not have viewed their homeland as more important ecologically than any other place on earth. I think they would have seen the rich biodiversity of the area as an abundance that enabled them to share with more living beings and communities—and therefore we have political relationships and the sharing of land with the Haudenosaunee and Wendat. I think they would have viewed zones of transition, whether a shoreline or an area between ecosystems, as gathering sites, sites of knowledge generation.

The ecosystems I was born into, and that form my body, are a boundary, a border between two separate and linked systems. On a macro scale, the boreal and mixed hardwood forests came together to create something new: a zone of overlapping presence that requires care, kindness, sacrifice and reciprocity to continue to bring forth a diversity and abundance of new life.

Of course, from the perspective of capitalism and the colonialism that fuels it, these overlapping zones of abundance are therefore territories rich in resources and capital. This is land that must be opened up to facilitate the material gain of a few elite white men; and thus the chain of lakes and rivers weaving its way through the centre of our home, from Chi'Nibish to Odawa Wikwedong (a Michi Saagiig Nishnaabeg name for Georgian Bay, I learned from Doug), and the veins and arteries leading to the lungs of the systems, the Great Lakes, needed to be choked off with a series of locks and canals in order to enable large boats to travel unhindered, taking loads of dead bodies to mills, furriers and smelters, and bringing loads of living white bodies to cut down, farm and occupy our overlapping and interlocking worlds while declaring them private property.

There are now forty-two locks covering 386 kilometres of waterways in the Trent-Severn system, giving Parks Canada complete control over the water level throughout the areas affected.

And the impact has been devastating on Kina Gchi Nishnaabeg ogamig, and on all the life that makes up our home formation; and these effects have been felt for hundreds of years. The Trent-Severn Waterway has destroyed the abundance of minomiin, the wild rice that was the foundation of our food and therefore our economic system, and that provided the fuel for migrating ducks, geese and birds to make the long journey across the big lake.

Fluctuating water levels flooded gravesites and marshes, and altered the biodiversity of shorelines. Eels and fish that relied on travel through aquatic ecosystems have died out. Bullfrogs have declined. And all these losses alter our relational practices, the ones that bring life together. We no longer smoke fish, because we don't have access to the fatty fish required for this.

Meanwhile, the lock system not only depleted things, it brought other things into our homeland. It brought millions of settlers and the infrastructure of settlement. The route from the Atlantic to the St. Lawrence through the Great Lakes to the west was valuable, because it could facilitate capitalism and bring its world-ending consequences farther west and north.

I learned our word for shoreline from Maddy's sister, Michi Saagiig Nishnaabe artist Olivia Whetung. Her piece *tibewh* means a body of water, or a shoreline you are in or on,[57] or it is a word that refers to the shoreline if you are seeing it from in the water.[58] The word suggests the idea of shoreline as understood not from my land-based existence but from the perspective of my ancestors who used the lakes and rivers to travel. In another shift in perspective, Whetung uses images from Google Maps—a bird's-eye view—to bead all forty-two locks of the Trent-Severn Waterway on squares of canvas.[59] The metallic beads form the water, while the edge where they meet the canvas is the lines of the locks.

I remember seeing *tibewh* in 2017, when it was installed in our local artist-run centre, and I was struck by the number of locks, each uniquely built to restrict and dominate a particular shoreline between Lake Ontario and Georgian Bay. At first encounter I remember struggling to find references in the images to the physical features of the locks I knew. I was looking for the shapes of the locks, particularly the mammoth Lock 21 in the city that towers over the water and landscape. But I couldn't find the columns in the images because I was assuming that Whetung had beaded the concrete structures. She hadn't. She'd beaded the water, and she'd beaded it from a bird's-eye perspective. Whetung asked me to see the water despite the locks. The water that, despite everything, is still here. Still coping and trying and flowing. Still moving.

In the summer of 2015, Maddy went on a solo canoe trip, paddling from the swamp in her mother's backyard that leads out into Chemong Lake, around the peninsula that is Curve Lake First Nation, through the Bobcaygeon lock, to the area that was described by her great-grandfather, in 1923 Williams Treaty meetings, as Whetung harvesting territory.[60] She was retracing the route of her family and her ancestors in order to try to understand the complications of enacting Nishnaabeg laws in this densely settled context, where private property runs right up the water's shoreline.

Maddy, her sister and I—we are all, in our various and different ways, trying to understand how Nishnaabeg thinking and practice lives in, through and around capitalism. Just as Doug did too. And all of us, through our various practices, fields of study and lives, are brought to the shore.[61]

Agaming: On the Shore

A little less alone.

Doug died in the summer of 2022, and part of my grieving has been to make an accounting of the importance of this attachment—and an accounting of regret, for all the things we didn't get to do together. The violence of dispossession has made access to Elders and land and Nishnaabe knowledge scarce, and that is why the death of such Elders is not merely a loss of parental or grandparental relationships; it is also the loss of bodies of knowledge that are difficult to recover. These are losses compounded by colonialism. When an Elder dies, there are things they saved in their body that you can't get back because they don't exist anywhere else in the world.

In the months leading up to his death, Doug and I talked a lot about Michi Saagiig Nishnaabeg beliefs and practices around the transition from physical and spiritual being to a solely spiritual one. Doug was spending more time in the spiritual world as his body retreated. And as he spent more time in this interstitial space, the space in between life and death, I was dragged there with him, reluctantly. It was difficult for me to stay present where the physical and spiritual worlds overlapped because I didn't want to feel the feelings invoked there. Yet this in-between space demanded my presence. It demanded I face my emotions. It demanded that I let go of the relationship Doug and I had for years, that of student and teacher, and be open to a sort of companionship at the end during a radical transformation: death.

During this time, Doug liked to recount what he thought would happen as he made his way to the spiritual world. He talked about the visiting he would do in the first four days; and the visiting he would do over that first year of fragility. He described the canoe, like the ones we'd seen etched into the rock at Kinomagewapkong, that would take him north, not west as most Nishnaabeg believe, across the water and into the skyworld.

Over the years we had both spent a lot of time in canoes because, of course, our people are lake people, and travelling by canoe, floating and being held by water, was the primary way our people moved through our territory. In the fall, Doug would sit in the front of his green canoe with a shotgun, hunting geese, and I would sit in the stern, trying to steer and paddle and follow all his instructions. Canoes require you to be in alignment with the water that is holding you. They require an awareness of currents and flow, and they provide a different orientation to the world than that of land. Canoes require intimacy with the shore. Travelling by water, whether it was by canoe in the spring, summer and fall or over the ice in the winter, was the primary way my ancestors moved around. This vantage point, floating on top of water, seeing the edges of water meeting land and land meeting sky, was an organizing force. Shorelines where land and water meet, where birds, fish and mammals meet, are zones of overlapping worlds, often teeming with diversity and mino-bimaadiziwin.

I'm wondering now what I would have learned if I'd built a birchbark canoe and used that to travel to Pinery Road and Concession 11 from my home in Nogojiwanong. What if I had been able to travel to this spot without using the *concession* roads that bisect and enclose the land?

The preparations and planning would likely have had to begin a year in advance, because I don't know how to build a canoe. I would have had to call Chuck Commanda from Kitigaan Ziibi and engage in some international diplomacy to ask for help.

Then I would have harvested birchbark in minookima, the second part of spring, when the broad leaves are born. And I would have needed to harvest the materials of four other trees: zesegaandagwadab (spruce roots), giizhikatig (cedar), mananoons (ironwood) and baapaagigun (ash). I would have obtained consent from each of these beings to help, and to do so I'd have needed the semaa I made from four different plants and dried last summer. Some of these materials are no longer easy to find in my territory, so I would have had to think about why that is so, name this and understand it, and then engage in more international diplomacy with the Dene to ask them for spruce gum. Maybe I'd have traded them some maple syrup or minomiin.

I would then have needed ten days to build the canoe, which would mean borrowing an Elder's front yard on the reserve and bringing in like-minded Nishnaabeg to help me.

At this point, I would have discovered I needed paddles. So I'd have found someone with knowledge, harvested the materials and built the paddles.

I would then have needed goodness knows how long to learn how to drive that thing.

Next, I would have asked the Elder whose lawn I was borrowing to build the canoe how to get to where I wanted to go. He would tell me:

Jackson Creek
Chemong
Buckhorn
Pigeon Lake
Sturgeon Lake
Cameron Lake
Burnt River

He would tell me where I needed to put offerings. Sure, as an act of reciprocity and acknowledgement of those living things that I was encountering, but also as a way of feeding into the network a burst of energy and goodwill.

This is a journey I would have liked to take with that Elder, but I should have thought of it decades ago. His body can no longer make the trip in a canoe; maybe a motorboat or a Ski-Doo if the lakes froze enough that year. And even then, I don't know.

I would have had to think carefully about water, because it's not safe to drink the water out of these lakes. I would have thought carefully about food as well. There would be layers of safety concerns: boat traffic, Jet Skis, racism, mosquitoes, sunburns, heat exhaustion, and resting points that aren't on private property—or maybe are on private property.

I think of Nanabush, who made a similar journey in a canoe at the beginning of time. I would merely have been

re-enacting something they did; something that generations of my ancestors did before me, and that, through this
re-enactment, I'd have been gifting those yet to be born.
Nanabush's journey was a struggle, an ordeal even, and they
relied upon countless beings for help. They almost didn't
make it, but this was also their method for learning about
the world in which Gzhwe Manidoo had placed them.

Reattachment, I think now, is not glamorous or romantic. I would have learned some beautiful things from my
re-enactment, but I also understand that some things are lost
that I can't get back. The densely populated route I would
have travelled would be a constant struggle. I would not
feel safe, not for one second, on this journey. And there is
a good chance my work of reattachment would have led to
feelings of alienation. I feel sick thinking about it.

In the summer of 2018, two Nishnaabekwewag, Tia
Cavanagh and Maddy Whetung, organized a birchbark
canoe–building session on Doug's front lawn in Curve Lake.
It was specifically curated to be welcoming and meaningful to Indigenous femmes and queers, and it was a space to
embody and practise consent. Every relationship is founded
upon a shared consent in Nishnaabeg thought. Working
with trees, water and fire to weave together strength and
gentleness means that when you are working with these
beings, you cannot force them. Force results in snapped ribs,
cracking birchbark, spliced spruce roots. In canoe building,
consent and accountability are practices embodied moment
to moment, and they serve to allow us to build deeper relationships with one another. This is preventive.[62]

About a month after Doug died, Maddy and I took our
kids to harvest cattails in a marsh inside the nature areas of

Trent University beside the Otonabee. The day was hot. We were sad. I was joking that we were orphans, and since Doug had passed, we only had Google and YouTube to figure out how to weave the long leaves into mats. My kid knew exactly where to take us because she had spent the most time of any of us in the Trent nature areas while at forest school. We put our offerings down. Then we picked the long leaves and hauled them back to Maddy's car.

Maddy used the cattails to teach us about shorelines as connectors as we wove warming mats and built the walls of shelters from what we had harvested. She told us that the roots and pollen of the cattails are food, and the fluff is used as insulation and to stuff pillows, while the gel found within the layers can be used to soothe skin irritations. The place where we harvested the cattails was a marsh, and I wouldn't have described it as a shore until I had this experience. Now I know that marshes are tiny shores, where the division between land and water breaks down. Cattails brought us to the shore that day. They connected us to water, land, bugs and each other. They also connected us to Doug.

Some medicine people describe cattails as the "defenders of the shoreline" because they prevent erosion, and Maddy told us that this description comes from our language.[63] In *Braiding Sweetgrass*, Potawatomi botanist Robin Wall Kimmerer retells a story of taking her biology students to harvest cattails as part of a university class she was teaching. Kimmerer writes about the biology of the plant and how it is adapted specifically for the winds and waves of shorelines, with an extensive network of rhizomes below the surface and no distinct stem. Instead, the stalk consists of a rolled bundle of leaves, sheathed around each other in concentric layers because no one leaf alone could withstand the wind and waves of the shore.[64]

Once again, this time through an understanding of the cattail, we see that a shoreline is a relational space mediating between worlds and beings.

And now I think that what I would have learned on my canoe trip to Pinery Road and Concession 11 is about shorelines, which are hard to map or comprehend on paper because they are made up of fractal geometry formed by other natural forces.

A fractal is a pattern that repeats forever, and every part of the fractal at every scale looks similar to the structure of the whole. Fractals, which can be found everywhere in nature, from snowflakes to mountains to networks of rivers to blood vessels, are also found in shorelines.[65] And in this way, the shoreline orients us: what we do on a small scale is how we exist at the large scale.

The shore is a space of overlapping or interconnected worlds, of edges and zones and areas of intensive transition. In the lakes and rivers of Kina Gchi Nishnaabeg ogamig, shores are places of diversity and abundance, places in which my ancestors would have spent a lot of their time—building homes, harvesting cattails, rice, berries, and aquatic plants and medicines, hunting and fishing. They were places of meeting, decision-making, ceremony and diplomacy. They were places of beginnings of life and of journeys and of deaths and of homecomings.

They continue to be places where we learn to be careful—the last places to freeze up in the fall and the first places to thaw in the spring. And they continue to be sites of constant transformation. As cottagers and homeowners build sandy beaches, decks, docks, lawns and retaining walls, the shoreline resists taking back any tiny space to begin to regrow. As cottagers and homeowners use herbicide, Michi Saagiig Nishnaabeg, ducks, geese and fish replant. As land-owners rope off, curate and alter, birds, fish, insects and Nishnaabeg violate.

For life forms that spend their time on the land, the shoreline is a passage to the water world; and for life whose entire world is water, the shoreline is world-ending, a foreign place that cannot provide the necessities to thrive. But for those species that live on the shoreline, the littoral zone is their world. Land, air and water mix in an overlapping beginning and ending.

Whenever I'm in a canoe, I'm struck by the shift in orientation that takes place. Travel by road and trail becomes travel by floating on the surface of rivers and lakes, arriving and departing from the shore. I notice space and light that doesn't exist in the same way in the bush. There is wind, and the consequences of wind. My canoe is on the surface or the edge of the water, and also on the surface and the edge of the skyworld, of air. My visual field shifts from the browns and greens of various textures in the forest to large swaths of blues, first in the sky and then reflected in the water. There is no escaping or finding shelter from the sun or the wind or the rain. There is no escape from the mosquitoes and blackflies. It is only at the shore that I can find shelter from the elements. It is only at the shore, the meeting of forest and lake, that I can rest.

We often put an offering in the water before we push off from the shore in our canoes. The shore is a place to set up camp, to gather water and harvest food. It is a place where

families come together in the summer to celebrate and
honour with ceremonies and feasting. It is where we come
to cool ourselves down, escape the bugs, clean ourselves,
just as the moose do. In the winter, frozen shorelines lead
us by foot, dog team or Ski-Doo into territory where we
cannot travel in the summer. The ice holds our fish camps
and our nets. In the spring, shorelines lead us to muskrat
push-ups and the first ducks and geese migrating home.

Shorelines are continually changing, mapping a coming together of land and water, and then unmapping the
departures. They are gathering sites for living beings from
the lake, the air and the land. They are sites of dense relationality, renewing relationships, reaffirming connections
and generating ecosystems.

In 2019, Candice Hopkins and Tairone Bastien curated
the first Toronto Biennial of Art, which brought together
artists from all over the world and asked them to consider
"The Shoreline Dilemma." This, they write, occurs when
scientific conventions break down in the face of the complexity of nature.[66] Indigenous peoples have long revered
the complexity of the earth and the ecosystems we live in,
and the Shoreline Dilemma reminds me that my ancestors,
too, understood the limits of human understanding and
therefore the ongoing implications of colonial systems we
currently struggle against.

Colonial interference places shorelines under tremendous pressure. Colonial societies exploit the gifts of shorelines by building cities, ports, harbours, causeways and roads
along them, using rivers and lakes as political borders and
places to expel waste water and effluent from the land.
At the same time, the shore is coveted by campers and

cottagers, which leads to waterfronts stacked with private property in the form of cottages, homes, condominiums, industrial development and even parkland.

The forces of this dispossession are intense and arresting.

Hopkins and Bastien write that shorelines are also, inherently, about resistance. The shore isn't bound by the same conventions as land or water or the skyworld. Shorelines resist conventional mapping—they are ever-shifting, fractal, they have no well-defined perimeter and evade attempts at quantification. Shorelines embrace the unknown, the unquantifiable and the fugitive. They resist systems that seek discipline and control.

In the fall of 2022, as part of my work at the Dechinta Centre for Research and Learning, I coordinated a land-based course on sovereign creative Indigenous artistic practice, focusing on the idea of shorelines. The class spent a week with Dene Elders and land-based practitioners, making things and living on Mackenzie Island in Tı̨ndeè, or the big lake, living at the shore and surrounded by shoreline. Dene have built camps on the island for many generations because it provides a safe place to shelter.

I'm thinking of that time now, remembering how the shore during the course was bursting with life. We were gathered in canvas tents and lived and worked together. In the mornings, students would leave the shore in motorboats to hunt ducks and fish the net with Elders, returning to camp with a blue plastic bin full of whitefish, jackfish or pike—and, if they were lucky, trout. Another Elder would teach them to fillet the fish to feed the camp or to make dry fish for later. One of our staff would take the extra fish and distribute them to the community while putting the guts and bones on another, nearby island for birds to eat. Students picked cranberries and Labrador tea, while Inuk instructor Krista Ulujuk Zawadski taught them how to make sewing needles out of duck bones. Secwépemc artist Tania Willard helped them use the materials around them to deepen their creative practices and relationship to the shore. Students canoed around the circumference of the island to learn a different perspective. I asked students to spend quiet time sitting on the shore, just listening. I noticed only a few minutes would go by before we would hear the laughter of children or Elders from camp. One evening an eagle fished outside our tents for nearly an hour.

I realize now that what I'm still learning from Doug, and also from Maddy's work on shorelines, from Olivia's work with the Trent-Severn Waterway, and from the land, is that these zones of overlap that bring together the water world and the land world, the Great Lakes, the St. Lawrence Lowlands and the boreal forest, are rich sites of mino-bimaadiziwin. They are rich sites of regeneration. They are rich sites of synergistic knowledge. At the shoreline and in this ecotone, this brings forth more life—in contrast to the colonial way, which always ends and diminishes life.

I add this knowledge to what I continue to learn from snow: that when you arrive, you make bonds.

Bullfrogs, Cattails and Water Lilies

To begin to sinter.

Stoney Lake in mid-June is gorgeous, with its rocky outcrops embraced by mature white pine. It is the gem of the Kawarthas—but it's not a place where I've spent much time because its beauty and proximity to Toronto means that it is prime cottage country (although *cottage* is a term used a little liberally here). These summer homes are mansions along the shoreline, the lots alone worth millions of dollars. The only place I might see another Nishnaabeg is on the tiny public beach sandwiched between dream homes.

This weekend, I've rented an Airbnb here—something that was more expensive than I could have ever imagined. Still, I'm here on a borrowed dock, in a bay full of lily pads and lily roots, remembering the shoreline. I'm visiting the place that made me, less than thirty minutes away from where I currently live—and I say "visiting" because, despite many degrees and good jobs, my family can't afford to live on the shore of Stoney Lake. We can't even really afford a weekend here in the off-season.

Paddling around the bay last night, I saw geese and goslings, a deer and a fawn, a beaver and an osprey, and all night long the bullfrogs were calling to each other in low, glugging tones. It's such a strange sound to hear in choir. There are lots of songbirds singing in the morning. The moon, somewhere between half and full light, a pathway on the lake.

It's early in the season, so these sounds are not drowned out by motorboats and Jet Skis. It's the sounds that strike me this morning, sounds that in the city I'd only hear on a recording manufactured to encourage me to relax. My mind must recalibrate what to do with these sounds; the choir is too complicated for my human brain to find structure and pattern. I want to hear the sounds and not block them out as background noise. I want to stay in that middle, meditative place.

The molecules that make up the water in Stoney Lake are closer together than the air molecules, and this means that the sound of the bullfrogs, Chi'denden, travels faster and more easily across it. Of course, this is why people sitting at the shore can hear the conversations in the canoe in the middle of the lake—and we think of the lake as an amplifier in this sense. Except it technically isn't amplifying anything; the molecules are just closer, more connected, and the transmission of the sound is faster than when the sound travels through air to my human ears, which have perfectly evolved to hear sounds travelling through air. This is why I feel surrounded, or engulfed, by frequencies created by this community of bullfrogs.

Doug passed into the spirit world when he was eighty years old, and for the five years leading up to his death he talked a lot about dying. He knew it was coming, and he prepared and thought it through. I didn't like talking about it and I wasn't very . . . well, present. It was too painful to imagine. A few years ago, the two of us were driving around the north part of Stoney Lake, just to be there. He talked about how this used to be an area where deer would gather for the winter. He would stop the truck periodically and we would walk across private property and alongside fancy houses, feeling both in awe of the architecture and humiliated, angry to be trespassers on our own land. One time we saw a wolf on the ice. As I write, I think this is the sort of sentence that will likely get edited out when I read through this later, because I have nothing else to say about the wolf or seeing it. It is a clear memory, though, of Doug and me: stopping the truck, looking out on the ice for nothing in particular and seeing another being. Another being dispossessed and humiliated. Also still here, moving over thin ice and private property, wondering what to do next.

Doug and I often talked about going bullfrog hunting, especially in the days before the Williams Treaty settlement, when this was the only Treaty Right the government recognized.[67] We never did, though, because Doug was concerned about the decline of frogs in our territory. He would always start talking about frogs by recounting how the sound of frogs mating in June had disappeared from the Kawarthas—first from Buckhorn and Chemong, and then from the other lakes.[68] He worried about the ongoing climate catastrophe, the fantastical destruction of wetlands and shorelines in which bullfrogs lived, and he taught me that, ethically, harvesting even one frog under these conditions was not only wrong, it would also break his heart. So we never did.

Several times, mostly in June, Doug would tell me the story of his famous bullfrog harvest—a story that is recorded as *R. v. Taylor and Williams* in the Ontario Court of Appeal.

Here is that story: Wayne Taylor, Doug, who was then Chief of Curve Lake, and Doug's seven-year-old son Keesic were fishing for bullfrogs on Crowe Lake when one of the tourist lodges on the lake called the Ministry of Natural Resources to report "Indians are fishing." This happened to Doug many times, and it has happened to me many times, and it has happened to my children several times as well. The times when it happened to me and Doug together, I can barely remember; I accepted this settler surveillance protection— of both their private property and their commons—as a normal part of land-based practice in our territory. The times it happened with my kids are seared not only into my memory but into the cells of my body.

Leaks.
Ricing.
Ricing.
Ricing.

The faces of those settlers when they called the police on our language nest as we were singing, gathered around a fire.

For years, Doug had said that if he ever got charged, he would fight it in court. So, on June 11, 1977, when he was in the front of a canoe on Crowe Lake, with Keesic in the middle and Wayne Taylor in the stern, and game wardens in a "square stern canoe" showed up, he knew he would fight. Using the minutes of the 1818 treaty, a lawyer and a strategy, he eventually won us, the descendants of the signatories of the 1818 treaty, the right to hunt bullfrogs. This was won in the Ontario Court of Appeal. And I'm thinking of that fight and that victory as I'm listening to the frogs this morning.

The sound of my choir of bullfrogs, calling in mates from the marshy shoreline of the bay, is louder than you may be thinking. Bullfrogs are known to have very large tympana, or eardrums, and their calls can be heard by mates hundreds of metres away. Some nights, the sound of bullfrogs along the shore dominates; you can't hear anything else. This is what is happening at the Airbnb on Stoney Lake. I don't need Rebecca Belmore's instrument to hear; I can't hear anything else from dusk until dawn. It is spectacular, and while I'm sure I've heard this chorus before, I don't remember those times the way I'm remembering this time.

Part of the reason the sound of bullfrog choirs in the summer has been rare in my life is that wetlands are now rare in my territory. I consulted the Ojibwe People's Dictionary for the Nishnaabeg words for wetlands. I typed in *wetlands*, then *marsh*, then *bog*, and finally *swamp*. The term *swamp* brought me the Nishnaabe word *mashkiig*, and I recognize *mashkiki* as the word for medicine.

I understand swamp as the place of medicine. I know that my people would have used this name partly because of the sheer number of plants in wetlands that they used as medicines. I remember harvesting lily root in wetlands around Hollow Water First Nation with Elder Garry Raven. I think now of harvesting rat root in swamps with Doug. These were always memorable occasions because I had to get out of the canoe while it was on the water, step in what felt like metres of sediment and reach down to harvest the roots. I remember the overwhelming pungent smell of stagnant water and decomposing organic matter. And of course, I think of harvesting wild rice in those same marshes, alongside ducks and geese, my kids screaming because they were covered in all kinds of insects. Mashkiig, an overlapping of the terrestrial and water worlds, are sites of tremendous life. I think of the shoreline full of ducks, geese, ospreys and herons; fish, frogs and turtles; muskrats, beavers, minks and deer; mosquito larvae and dragonfly nymphs; lily pads and wild rice; and stagnant, decaying organic matter. I think of ecosystems that remove pollutants from water and get rid of 90 percent of water-borne pathogens. Ecosystems that clean the groundwater we rely on to drink. Ecosystems that sequester carbon and hold water like sponges buffering against flooding.[69]

Capitalism understands otherwise.

In southern Ontario, between 70 percent and 90 percent of original wetlands have been destroyed—draining these worlds for farmland, settlement, industrial development and highway construction. On a planetary scale, we've lost one-third of global wetlands in the last forty-five years.[70] The threats don't stop there, though. Pollution, climate change and the artificial modification of water levels—like that which occurs in the management of the Trent-Severn Waterway—also contribute to the desecration.[71]

All of this makes my bullfrog choir even more important. I know that entire worlds exist at the same time and in the same place as me in this moment. The sound waves from the very air we share vibrate over their vocal cords and disrupt the summer night. They scream to me that I don't need to remake the world; I need only to figure out how to fit into the cascading networks of life that I'm already part of, in a way that doesn't destroy this bullfrog choir.

"Remembering Where It Used to Be"[72]

Out in the bush one day, Doug started telling me about eels. I didn't know what he was talking about, because there are no eels in our territory and there is no ocean in our territory. I knew from my biology days that there are sea lampreys in the Great Lakes—but these are not even really eels. And this was definitely not what Doug was talking about. Doug was telling me about a time when American eels, who originate in the Sargasso Sea in the Atlantic, migrated through the St. Lawrence River and Lake Ontario and into the lakes, rivers and creeks in our territory. He was talking about an abundance of eels I couldn't comprehend, saying how they were an important source of protein and medicine for our people.

I tried to map out that migratory route in my head: Stoney Lake, Otonabee, Rice Lake, Trent River, Lake Ontario, St. Lawrence, Atlantic Ocean, Sargasso Sea. Fresh water to salt water. Michi Saagiig Nishnaabeg to Mohawk to Mi'kmaq to Taíno to the Caribbean, the middle passage, west coast of Africa, northern part of South America . . . the Pacific, Naarm, the world.

Every year, Doug said, the eel came into our homeland as a messenger, telling us that our world making was deeply connected not just to the species we shared our immediate time and space with, but to peoples and forms of life all over the world, on the land, in the water and in the sky.

And the eels carried knowledge in their bodies about their part of the world, or the ocean. If the eels were abundant and healthy, it told people something about the health of their environment and the travel route. It told us something about ourselves as well. If the eels were scarce or thin or sick, then maybe we needed to ease off harvesting and rely on other beings for sustenance. The same knowledge came from the birds and all the great migrators.

Immersing myself in Anishinaabe thought was how I grounded myself in the now, and I understood that because of the dispossessions colonialism had subjected me to, I needed to spend time recovering this knowledge. The eels tell me, though, that my responsibilities don't stop there; they aren't so insular. I am called to bring this knowledge into conversation with those who are engaged in different but related anti-colonial struggles in my neighbourhood and beyond.

Today, water is teaching me that any meaningful Anishinaabe world making requires not only the radical transformation of the Anishinaabe out from under the domination of colonialism but the radical transformation of the state, and the planetary abolition of racial capitalism with its heteropatriarchal violences and structures that naturalize and reproduce the hierarchies it needs to replicate itself on earth.

Such world making requires the profound reorganization of everything.

For me, the ocean is something distant and planetary. It's not within the intimate sphere of my homeland, and I don't have a direct relationship with it; I don't feel, hear or see the ocean on a regular basis. Whenever I'm around the ocean, it seems foreign to me, with its salt and strange smells and vastness. Our word for sea or ocean is *Gchi Gaming*—and this is also our name for Lake Superior, which means, literally, "big lake." Still, I understand that while my ancestors might not have experienced the Atlantic Ocean directly, they were in close relationship to American eels that came from the ocean.

Gchi Ziibing, "big river," as my ancestors called the St. Lawrence River, connects the Atlantic Ocean to Lake Ontario, and these waterways connect Michi Saagiig Nishnaabeg to the Mohawks and the Algonquin peoples as our neighbours. It is through these waterways that we are connected to the eels too. I've only seen glimpses of eels a few times, but Doug had vivid memories of bays in Stoney Lake teeming with eels. He remembered the fatty taste and how much his Elders cherished the eels. Henry Lickers, a Mohawk Knowledge Holder from Akwesasne, tells us that for Mohawks, eels were a very important source of nutritious food that was easy to transport. Their skins were dried and used as bandages, as a medicine to relieve rheumatism, and as wraps on the handles of tools to provide grip. Their fats were used to waterproof clothing, and their oils to cure earaches.[73] Algonquin Elder William Commanda used to talk about silver pathways in the moonlight as rivers teemed with eels migrating upstream. He affirmed the oral traditions of the Mohawks and the Michi Saagiig Nishnaabeg while he was working with Ontario's American Eel Recovery Program when he said, "[they were] plentiful beyond imagination."[74]

My ancestors knew eels as a regulator and a cleaner of aquatic ecosystems, creating a balance within fish com-

munities. They are what Western scientists call a keystone
species—a species on which other species in an ecosystem
largely depend, such that if it were removed, the ecosystem would change drastically. They are also shape-shifters
or transformers, born as eggs in the Sargasso Sea, east of
Bahamas and southwest of Bermuda. This is where they
breed. (Scientists have never witnessed this one-time mating, and they simply assume that the eels die afterwards.[75])
Eggs hatch into larvae that are called leptocephali—a trans-
parent and willow-leaf-like form. The larvae travel with
the Gulf Stream system for seven to twelve months, transforming into glass eels once they reach fifty-five to sixty-
five millimetres in length. Glass eels become progressively
pigmented as they move across continental shelves to the
shoreline. Once pigmented, they are considered elvers. The
elver stage lasts from three to twelve months, during which
time some migrate upstream into fresh water. In Atlantic
Canada, timing of elver migration varies geographically. On
the north shore of the Gulf of St. Lawrence, arrival occurs
in July, when elvers reach sixty to seventy millimetres in
length. As elvers grow, they become known as yellow eels,
and after a few years they mature into silver eels. Some silver
eels return to the Sargasso Sea to reproduce—a 4,500-kilo-
metre swim away.[76]

When elvers used to arrive in our territory in the
spring, they would bring with them news of the ocean in
physical ways, through the size of their communities and
the health of their bodies, and in spiritual ways, through
prayer, dreaming and ceremony with the Nishnaabeg. And
when silver eels arrived back in the ocean, they would take
the news of our freshwater environment with them as well,

using the same means. And so, when fewer and fewer eels returned to Michi Saagiig Nishnaabeg ogamig, we knew something was very wrong. And when fewer and fewer eels returned to the ocean, beings there knew something was very wrong too.

Eels once made up half the biomass in Lake Ontario.

American eels are contingents, meaning there is a diversity of life cycles within the same species. This diversity makes them resilient. Some eels live their entire lives in the ocean. Others migrate to fresh water and spend ten to twenty-five years in ponds, streams, rivers, lakes and marshes. Sex differentiation is determined by fish density: the greater the density, the more females develop.[77] In Ontario, most of the eels are female, and many are "old females," or aunties and grandmothers—they hold knowledge and experience and embody eel oral tradition. This makes the community more resilient, because the older females are wise and teach the younger community members how to live and how to survive. Most of these Kokums are found at the upper limits of the migratory routes.[78]

American eels in Ontario are endangered, which means they are facing imminent extinction or extirpation. Eels started to feel the death drive of capitalism early on; the hydro dams, generating stations with turbines, man-made barriers like locks and seaways all made travelling the St. Lawrence River dangerous and difficult. Today there are over eight thousand dams in the St. Lawrence watershed.[79] Commercial overfishing by settlers at the end of the nineteenth century and the beginning of the twentieth led to population crashes. Pollution and declining water quality combined with habitat loss didn't help things either.

Doug Williams remembered an abundance of eels when he was a kid in the 1940s and 1950s. In the 1980s, eels travelling in the St. Lawrence during the fall dropped from 25,000 a day to 250 a day.[80]

In Mohawk territory, Henry Lickers tells us, the construction of the Moses–Saunders hydro power dam as part of the St. Lawrence Seaway between 1954 and 1958 was catastrophic for eels. He remembers the band council sending trucks and wagons to collect the dead and rotting bodies of thousands of eels, piled to half a metre deep, in the bays and coves downstream of construction.[81] "It was horrible to see," said Lickers in a 2008 interview with the *Walrus*.[82] Meanwhile, Algonquin Elder Commanda reports a 99 percent reduction in his watershed from the 1970s. A catastrophic world ending, with cascading consequences.

In *Undrowned: Black Feminist Lessons from Marine Mammals*, Alexis Pauline Gumbs takes on Western science and the world it has built around marine mammals, a world that tries to govern how humans think about, relate to and interact with our siblings in the ocean. Guidebooks to our physical world, for example, and the science they present or summarize, manage our relationships with the natural world even as they are rooted in a world view that entrenches hierarchy, is motivated by human ambitions, and sees non-human forms of life as resources to fuel the machines of capitalism. Western science is not objective, or valueless, but a thought system with a particular history that has been tied to colonialism, genocide and anti-Blackness throughout our history. In the era of anti-vaxxers and anti-science thinkers, I feel a heightened need to be careful about how I critique Western science. What a few years ago could have been insightful, bringing attention to how the scientific method erases Indigenous Knowledge systems or how every knowledge system, even Western science, has its assumptions and limits, now seems dangerous.

Alexis writes that, as a mammal, as a "Black woman ascending with and shaped by a whole group of people who were transubstantiated into property and kidnapped across an ocean," she is attracted to the wonder of marine life as kin. But when she went to the aquarium with her guidebooks, she found languages of deviance and denigration, awkward binary assignments of biological sex, and a criminalization of animals that escaped the gaze of biologists. She found herself confronted with the colonial, racist, sexist and hetero-patriarchal capitalist constructs that were trying to kill her.[83]

SARGASSO SEA

The eel, then, was a link between me and the Sargasso Sea nearly five thousand kilometres away. And my people once had long-term, intimate relationships with eels. They knew their stories and their travels up the big river to the big lake. They knew how important eels were in organizing aquatic ecosystems in our homeland.

And the world of the eel is made up of several very different, overlapping worlds: the ocean and a saltwater environment, and aquatic environments and the land. Like the shoreline. Like Michi Saagiig Nishnaabeg ogamig. Like sintering snow. I think once again that worlds existing in between spaces are diverse and generative places. Beings that travel between, build between, exist in interstitial spaces are portals to other worlds; and the portals themselves are worlds on their own, too.

I see, too, that the bodies, the life cycle and the world
of eels are valuable internationally, in a way that made these
living beings vulnerable to capitalist elimination. Their
bodies, like the bodies of beavers and white pine and the
Anishinaabeg, were used to fuel colonialism.

The bodies of eels are a map, just like the rings on the
flesh of a maple tree are a map. They map the life cycle
from egg to leptocephalus to glass eel to elver to yellow
eel to silver eel. Their bodies are archives of the physical
conditions of their world: water temperature, nutrients, the
quality of habitats, the productivity of their food webs, the
health of the ecosystems they live in and travel through, and
the effects of global climate change. The fat stores in their
bodies are a record of the contamination and pollution and
disease they encounter.

The Sargasso Sea is a sea with no shores. Its boundaries
are ocean currents: to the west is the Gulf Stream Current,
to the north is the North Atlantic Current, to the east is
the Canary Current, and to the south is the North Atlantic
Equatorial Current.[84] The only land in the sea is the island
of Bermuda. With ocean currents on all sides, the sea itself
is calm and warm, with stable weather conditions, and I'm
guessing this is why it is an ideal home for eels to mate. The
sea is also in motion, in the form of a subtropical gyre that
rotates in the same direction as the sun, clockwise. On the
surface of the sea is a mat of sargassum seaweed. This dense
mat is used by eels as their breeding ground. They share the
mat with fish and turtles. Wahoo, tuna and humpback whales
come here to forage. Young sea turtles travel to the safety
of the mat to grow.[85] The mat is a gathering site of many
forms of life. American eels bring back this intercommunal

experience, stories and knowledge to Mohawk, Algonquin, Mi'kmaq and Michi Saagiig Nishnaabeg peoples.

> Jackson Creek
> Chemong
> Buckhorn
> Pigeon Lake
> Sturgeon Lake
> Cameron Lake
> Pinery Road & Concession 11
> Burnt River
> Cameron Lake
> Trent-Severn Waterway
> Lake Ontario
> St. Lawrence River
> Gulf of St. Lawrence
> North Atlantic Current
> Sargasso Sea

Michi Saagiig Nishnaabeg worlds were enmeshed with the world of the eel. Capitalism all but ended the world of the eels in Nishnaabegaki, and this occurred within the span of my life.

What I know now about eels signals the danger of dividing knowledge into disciplines, geographic regions, time periods and particular struggles. Empire and capitalism are global, and when knowledge is enclosed, it is incomplete.

Maps to Statelessness

For my ancestors, flooding was a normal, everyday part of spring. As the snow was melting in March and April, the rivers and creeks filled up and often spilled their banks. The counterpoint to this was the dryness of late summer, when the creeks were reduced to a trickle and the forest was tinder. Life flowed with these natural cycles. My ancestors didn't gather on the flood plains during spring. They didn't try to canoe down shrunken creeks in August. And although there were times of scarcity, particularly in the winter, the land provided everything they needed, and the community made sure that everyone's needs were met.

These days, I'm carrying Doug's creation story around with me through the daily rhythms of my life. There are moments where I'm overwhelmed and I feel as though I'm drowning in problems with no solutions, in never-ending work tasks, and in feelings of helplessness as I watch Israel destroy every living being in Gaza. Feeling overwhelmed is a kind of existential flood. But as Steven Salaita writes, feeling helpless doesn't mean being useless.[86] I'm also thinking about Nibi and the decision they made to flood the earth after Gizhiigokwe and Gzhwe Manidoo's attempts at world making had failed. I think about how, when you travel the land with Elders and stop to set up camp, there is always shockingly little dialogue as each person does what needs to be done to make a home. Someone immediately starts gathering firewood to make a fire to boil tea. Someone else surveys the spot and determines the best place to set up tents or make the fire. Other people unload the canoe or the boat. They are embodying the same ethics as Nibi: they see a job that needs to be done, and they do it. A few years ago, I was teaching in the north at Dechinta and we had someone in our group who was struggling to follow the path into our main teaching cabin. The ground was uneven and there was no railing. One of our Elders observed this. The next day, he had built two steps up to the cabin. He saw the problem and he did what he could do to assist. Just like Nibi and their flood.

The gathering of animals floating in the flood with Gizhiigokwe, on the back of Chi'Mikinak, is not a Westphalian concept of state whereby a system of sovereignty is set up over a given area, or a monopoly of domination set over the land and the beings on the turtle's back. To do that would go against the responsibility to make worlds and bring forth more life. What Nibi, Gizhiigokwe and the animals did, along with Chi'Mikinak, was to sinter. They formed bonds and attachments.

They were surrounded by the edge of the turtle's shell— a shoreline of sorts—and so it was quite possible for them to build a Westphalian state; that was an option. They could have drawn *a line* around the turtle and elected someone to be the boss. They could have developed a system of rules and punishments for life on the turtle's back. They could have defended their border from other birds and animals that needed a place to rest and recuperate. All these were options open to them. But none would bring forth more life. None were world making. None were congruent with the ethics they had inherited from the skyworld.

If I were to draw a map of this moment in the story, what would it look like? It could be a map of a state, with a red line around the turtle's shell demarcating its borders. It could be a representation of the physical features of the shell. Or it could be a visual representation of relationships.

The yellow pond lily is a food and a medicine for Nishnaabeg. It is also a person with a spirit powerful enough to heal us, and I've known many medicine people to use the roots to treat various diseases. I've spent hours pulling up pond lily roots in knee-high sludge or diving below the surface of the water to wrestle whole roots from the sediment, so that these same Elders can process the pineapple-shaped lily roots into powdered medicines.

There are beautiful origin stories about how pond lilies came to live among us, and there are many tellings of these stories. A short version is that a star, or star person, fell so in love with the Nishnaabeg that they wanted to come and live among us. But they struggled in conversation with the people about what form of life to take and tried various ones. And they found that although they loved life in the physical world of the Nishnaabe, they missed life amongst the stars. They eventually settled on being the water lily, where they would spend summers close enough to the Nishnaabeg to see and hear us, and return to the star world for the winter months.

There's a lot to think about in this story: the expansion of the body beyond physical forms, the transformation of being from one form of life to another, and themes of presence, balance, boundaries and communication. There is gifting and sharing of time, space and one's own unique gifts.

Doug's not here, so I can no longer ask him about any of this. And while that's heartbreaking, it's also okay. I remember there came a point after I had finished the first draft of my book *As We Have Always Done* when Doug gently pushed me out of the nest. I was asking him to read another draft, and he was resisting because he felt it was time I took responsibility for my own ideas and thinking—not because he disagreed with them, but because they are ultimately my responsibility. This sort of letting go is a part of our knowledge too, and in the last ten years this pattern happened over and over as Doug passed along more and more responsibilities to me. He was preparing for his journey to the spirit world. I tell myself now that this is okay, even though the loss feels immense in a thousand different ways. The land and the water are still here, and they are the template for our knowledge.

Métis artist and activist Christi Belcourt's 2010 exhibition *Mapping Roots: Perspectives on Land and Water in Ontario* explored Indigenous practices of mapping through a series of paintings.[87] The curatorial essay that accompanied the exhibition explained how Indigenous maps are narratives of relationality and interconnection, not a set of fixed positions in space. Such maps existed in people's minds as memories and stories, personal, intimate, and based on embodied practice, experiential knowledge, dreams and oral tradition. Sometimes these mappings were written down on birchbark scrolls, scraps or hides, or in rock paintings and etchings. In the design of beadwork and Wampum. Scratched into sand, ash, snow and dirt. Most times, they were not written down at all. They were shared by travelling the route. They were shared through story.

The maps were an expression of relationship, of presence and of intimacy—so much so that in writing this, I wonder if *map* is even the right term.

There are two paintings in Belcourt's collection that stand out in my mind. One is a "map" of a water lily— a yellow pond lily, specifically.

Christi's painting encompasses or maps the stories, the teachings and ethics, and the themes I recognize from my own knowledge. Her mapping is not a fixed position in space, but a charting of the relationships that make up the water lily—the droplets of light from the sun, moon and star people around the edges of the leaves that catch the sun's light and convert it into food; the flower itself, literally a star in the lake, the edges of the water and arid worlds meeting at the surface and then again at the bottom; and the internal workings in the stem of the plant as connectors of air, water, light and soil, and as co-creators of life.

Water lilies belong at the shore. They are linked to the skyworld, the water world, the land and the air. Christi makes this visible to us through her art, even though to our ancestors it was likely both visible and normal in the world.

The second painting in the series that stands out for me is more in line with the standard definition of a map, although very few people would recognize it as such. The title of this painting is *Facing West*, and it appears to be a stylized Nishnaabe figure facing west, a figure with a spinal cord and lines indicating energy radiating from the head, as is so often seen on teaching rocks to denote a spiritual being.

Belcourt, though, wasn't just painting a figure in this work. She was painting and reinterpreting an old Nishnaabeg mapping of a canoe route, from the head of Lake Superior near Fort William travelling west and inland, to Lake of the Woods. A Nishnaabeg had shared their narrative of the route with a fur trader, and that fur trader had written it down. Nishnaabeg maps, after encountering European thinking, were oriented on an east-west axis.

This is similar to a work by Inuit artist Pudlo Pudlat called *The Settlement*. In it, Pundlat draws his home community situated on the land and in the clouds. In Inuit homelands, when the clouds are close to the ground, they can reflect the shifting surfaces of, for example, the land, bodies of water, villages or herds of caribou. Travellers would look at the clouds to see the forms up ahead, and to gauge distances.[88] This map of Pundlat's Inuit world included land, sky, water, clouds, caribou, people—a sort of mapping of the vertical instead of the horizontal. A glimpse of part of an Inuit network of life.

Anishinaabeg artist Bonnie Devine, in *Battle for the Woodlands: Anishinaabitude*, uses maple, red willow, twigs, paper, seagrass, buffalo hides, moose hide, felt, copper, nickel beads and shells along with acrylic and high-resolution digital files in a multimedia installation to reimagine an early nineteenth-century map of Upper and Lower Canada to reflect Anishinaabe world making. The five Great Lakes in the image are replaced with animals and spirits, which to me gestures towards Nishnaabeg territoriality, where caretaking responsibilities were split amongst Clans living in different parts of the territory. According to Doug, prominent Michi Saagiig Nishnaabeg Clans were caribou, eagle and crane, and I recognize Lake Ontario as a hooved Clan in Devine's depiction. The Clan system was a kind of organizing that tied particular peoples to territory and a set of relationships with other Nishnaabeg; and a link between the Nishnaabeg and the animal (and sometimes plant) world through Clan affiliation. Devine's map, in contrast to the original colonizers' map, documents these relationships. In it, she has decentred humans. She has drawn a depiction of Nishnaabeg "nationhood" beyond the form of a state.[89]

This leads me to Inuvialuk artist Maureen Gruben and her piece titled "We all have to go someday. Do the best you can. Love one another." In my work in Denendeh, I've heard Elders repeat, over and over, "Do the best you can" and "Love one another." The title and the piece come from her father, an Inuvialuk hunter who carried his land in his heart. In a conversation with Kyra Kordoski in *C Magazine*, Gruben tells the story of being in the hospital with her dad and looking at the results of his angiogram, identifying calcified parts. Gruben notes that his heart is in the north, travelling over Inuvialuit lands. She says, "When we talk about his life, we're talking about this land. He believed this was the best place on Earth, that we have everything that we need to live a good life here in Tuk[toyaktuk]. We have caribou, we have geese, we have all the fish we want."[90] Gruben noticed in her father's medical angiogram's path the pathways of caribou migration. In the art piece, or her map, she traces the angiogram onto tanned deer hide using a series of punched-out holes and embroidered knots, creating those migration paths. Gruben is telling me that the map of her father's heart is also the map of caribou migration.

To me, these are all glimpses of a map with no nation—
or, to put it a different way, these are all maps of Indigenous
statelessness.

WAMPUM

When my colleague Daniel Heath Justice moved from the
University of Toronto to the University of British Columbia, he gifted me a teaching Wampum of the Friendship Belt
between the Haudenosaunee Confederacy and the Nishnaabeg. A teaching Wampum is a replication of the original
Wampum for the purposes of teaching and sharing. I didn't
know very much about Wampum at the time, but I was
lucky, because many Nishnaabeg had worked hard to pull
that knowledge through and out of the grip of colonialism.

First, Doug helped me to understand the practice from
what he'd learned from his Curve Lake uncles Madden
and Makoons. And then the work of another friend, Alan
Ojiig Corbiere, an Odawa historian from M'Chigeeng First
Nation, professor, language speaker and Canada Research
Chair in Indigenous history of North America at York University, also helped me think about the belt. Alan has been
studying and researching Nishnaabeg history and treaties for
two decades, and he has an incredible knowledge of our
practice of Wampum. I love watching Alan's YouTube lectures, not only because I have a tremendous respect for his
work but because he is very funny. In one of my favourite
such lectures, Alan speaks, in English and Nishnaabemowin,
at Casino Rama in the territory of the Chippewas of Rama
First Nation, introducing the audience to four Wampum.
The second is the one that Daniel gave me—the Friendship Belt[91] between the Haudenosaunee and the Nishnaa-

beg. Alan explains that *belt* isn't quite the right word, since Wampum strings were not worn around the waist and used to hold in our stomachs, but rather over the shoulder in a diagonal fashion, sometimes with bags attached to the ends. He explains that our homelands or council fires or "nations" are often represented in Wampum by diamonds, hexagons, squares or rectangles. In the case of the Friendship Wampum, there is a rectangle at each end—one representing the Haudenosaunee and the other representing the Nishnaabeg. He tells us that the rectangles are often referred to as "mats," and that the two mats are joined with three long lines of white beads or shells. While four is an important number for Nishnaabeg, three is significant to the Haudenosaunee, and each row of beads represents peace, righteousness and the good mind. On my gifted replica, the three lines joining the two squares is ten times as wide as the rectangles themselves, indicating, to me at least, that the important part here is not the mats but the connection, the pathway composed of peace, righteousness and the good mind that is forged, nurtured and maintained between the two nations. When I look at the strings woven together, I think of the belt as a close-up view of one relationship or affinity in a network of living relations. The sea of white shells or beads tells of our relationships to plants, animals, birds, fish, insects, and waterways and landforms. Alan uses the phrase *Gchi-Miigis-apikan* to refer to the Wampum strings, explaining that *Miigis* is a name for the shells originally used in the strings. One interpretation of *apikan*, according to Alan, is "the message is the burden."[92] The process or struggle of being in communication, then, is the message, is the burden. It is the work and the labour.

Another map of Nishinaabeg statelessness.

It's hard to think of Indigenous statelessness, the refusal of the state, the refusal of Canada, without thinking about my Gchi-Miigis-apikan partners in general, and Mohawk women, and the work of Mohawk scholar Audra Simpson in particular. In the last chapter of *Mohawk Interruptus*, Simpson, in speaking about the 1990 resistance at Kanehsatà:ke, commonly known as the "Oka Crisis," writes:

> Iroquois women are too often and too easily
> imagined simply as "caretakers of the land" and
> "mothers of the nation" in a way that is stripped
> of its contemporary valences, instantiations and
> meaning, and in a way that disappears Two-Spirit,
> queer, trans and genderqueer people. As well,
> women are imagined in a way that occludes the
> ongoing effects of white, settler patriarchy in their
> communities and in their lives. With Oka we see
> the empirical face of that caretaking: women who
> called a peaceful protest and then an armed refusal
> against further dispossession. And we have there
> women who then *managed* that refusal during a
> seventy-eight-day armed standoff.[93]

There are countless examples of the Mohawk refusal of the state, from their lacrosse team refusing Canadian passports and travelling internationally on their own, to refusals of Indian Act governance and voting in Canadian elections in favour of the continuation of Longhouse governance, to the refusal of dispossession we witnessed during Oka in favour of Haudenosaunee visions of confederacy, nationhood and stateless political formations. These refusals are maps of Haudenosaunee statelessness, and an embodied understanding that the state is incompatible with Haudenosaunee life.

MINO–BIMAADIZIWINMAPPING

Mino-bimaadiziwin is both a concept and a living practice within Anishinaabeg thought. It is also a term overused by Anishinaabeg academics and writers, and by me—but I think about it a lot, and each year I think I understand it better, and so I continue to write and think alongside it, and to try to embody it. *Mino* is a prefix meaning that something is good or well, balanced, healthy. *Bimaadiziwin* is life, or the art of living, a process, a particular way, or ways, of living life.

The Anishinaabe or Ojibwe people's homeland is located roughly around the Great Lakes in Canada and the United States. I am from the eastern part of this territory, the Michi Saagiig Nishnaabeg, and our home is the north shore of Lake Ontario. Mino-bimaadiziwin was generated by my ancestors living in this region for tens of thousands of years and is often translated from my language as "the good life."

Translation is a powerful, political and oftentimes dangerous process for Indigenous peoples. Extracting a single concept or phrase out of our complex knowledge systems, taking it out of embodied practice and placing it in text, translating it, often literally, into English, and then repeating it in all kinds of different contexts results necessarily in dilution. As writers and academics (me included) cycle and recycle these artifacts, meaning can shift, and complex ways of world building can be reduced to paragraphs in studies, or to phrases, or even hashtags. Certain concepts academics latch onto take on an importance that they might not have

originally carried because they are now well known to out-
siders, and these same concepts can easily be re-coded to signal
all kinds of things within colonial societies. For instance,
mino-bimaadiziwin does not carry moralistic judgments
about what "living a good life" might entail—other than, in
my view, one that is against capital.

This is the weight of writing about mino-bimaadiziwin
when there are an endless number of other concepts in
Nishnaabemowin that could be used just as effectively as a
window into the complex thinking that builds Nishnaabeg
worlds in the present.

For me, the way through this dilemma is to centre the
land and land-based practice in my life and work. The land
has a way of levelling things, of cutting through what we
think we know, of forcing us to engage in the practices of
our peoples, knowing that our peoples are the priority. The
knowledge that has sustained my own people is generated
with the land, and from tens of thousands of years of practising living where the accumulation of wealth was thought
to be a mistake, the idea of property was seen as selfish,
borders were meant to be zones of decreasing presence, and
the overarching principle was that an individual must live in
such a way that they gave more than they took.

My favourite translation of *mino-bimaadiziwin* comes
from Winona LaDuke. She translates it as "continuous
rebirth": living life, individually, communally and globally,
in a way that brings forth more life, not just human life but
all life—that of plants, animals, rivers, lakes, oceans, streams,
insects, everything that is alive.[94]

Nishnaabeg concepts like this should be read and understood as windows into a very different way of organizing the

world. They are embedded in an ethical, legal and political system that is counter to racial capitalism and the systems it uses to organize life. For one thing, Nishnaabeg society is non-hierarchical and deeply relational. Place and time were, and are, endlessly shared with all forms of life so that both individual and communal needs are met. Human life isn't centred or placed above the life of the beaver, for example, or that of raspberries, or the forest. In fact, mino-bimaadiziwin ensures that Nishnaabeg life fits into the network of life that already exists on a planetary scale—the ecosystem—in a way that ensures the continuity of local and global living systems.

In Michi Saagiig Nishnaabeg life, the harvesting of minomiin, or wild rice, was one of those cyclical practices that were foundations of our bush economy. Families would come together, along with ducks, geese and migratory birds, at camps on the lakeshores in late summer and early fall to harvest the rice. In pairs, people would paddle canoes through the wild rice growing along the shoreline, one person gently knocking the grains of rice into the bottom of the canoe. Most of the grains would fall directly into the lake, reseeding the bed. Migratory birds would be plentiful in the rice, storing energy for their migration south for the winter. The harvest would be taken back to camp and families would work together over the next month, drying, parching, husking and winnowing the rice into a staple food that could easily be stored and would sustain families through the winter months. There were songs, stories and dances associated with the wild rice moon, and each year knowledge was generated and mobilized through the communal harvesting and processing. Ricing was an embodiment of the ethics of mino-bimaadiziwin, ethics that could also be applied to harvesting moose, picking blueberries or medicines, hunting geese, making maple sugar, or fishing at camp.

Mino-bimaadiziwin also grounds our politics, decision-making, leadership and governance. Taking another being's life so that one might feed oneself and one's family was not something done without thought, and so treaties between the Nishnaabeg and other forms of life, including humans, were maintained so that both nations would flourish.

Within this way of thinking, mino-bimaadiziwin builds a world that categorically rejects racial capitalism. It creates a society where an individual's or group's accumulation of wealth and property is seen as exploitation, an imbalance, something that over time leads to catastrophe within the network of life. It is an orientation that values and thrives on diversity and on individuals being their best selves. It is a system that continually generates the knowledge we need to propel the relation itself and to bring forth more life.

In my life, mino-bimaadiziwin compels me to build a different world, outside the one colonialism enforces. It compels me to do this in a relational fashion, and to seek out others who are doing different but similar world-building work locally and globally. It requires me to reject heteropatriarchy, anti-Blackness and human-centred thinking and practice. It requires me, and all of us, to dream of, envision and actualize ways of living outside our current imaginings, and to do this as a practice for generating the knowledge we need to reimagine the world.[95]

Rape
Dialogue
Negotiations
Starvation
Death
Relocation
Treaty
Residential Schools
Rape
Consultations
Litigations
Aboriginal Rights
Death
Self-Government
Modern Treaties
Rape
Inquiries
Royal Commissions
Reconciliations
Rape
Disappearance
Death
Certainty

Mino-bimaadiziwin is incommensurate with statehood because networks built from relationships are incommensurate with statehood. The nation of Canada presents itself to us as a colonial state, and it requires Indigenous peoples to present ourselves in the same way, not only refusing but destroying Indigenous systems of living inside the network of the planet. It destroys not only our governing and political formations but how we relate to one another and our most intimate relationships. The settler state initiated a set of laws, policies, regulations and societal norms intended to bring all living beings in line with its world-killing logics. At every turn, the state tries to map us into a controlled and diminished existence, using the language of recognition and rights, and making us think that without the state and without these rights, we will cease to exist as Indigenous peoples.

My people have tried very hard, for centuries, to ensure this does not happen. Treaties were meant to make things commensurable between a state and us. Christi Belcourt's water lilies teach me that nothing could be further from the truth. They are screaming Audra's articulation of Mohawk refusal.

"All of Them Carrying Yesterday"

Years ago, before I moved home and began working with Doug, I spent a lot of time in Hollow Water First Nation on the east side of Lake Winnipeg. While doing research there, I learned there were some birchbark scrolls at the Smithsonian Institute. They had been "collected" by anthropologist A. Irving Hallowell, who was working with communities in the area in the 1930s and 1940s. The scrolls were likely Mide, and the Elders in Hollow Water were interested in seeing them. So together we travelled to Washington, DC, to visit them. After we arrived in Washington and got settled into the hotel, the Elders wanted to go visit the river, to make offerings. It was raining, and so they sent me to a dollar store to get ten black garbage bags that would be their raincoats. Walking through Georgetown in our garbage bags is a memory that will always make me laugh.

We went to the river. The Elders prayed and made their offerings. Garry Raven Ban found a stick and wrapped blue cloth around it to hold tobacco, sending it floating out on the Potomac. When these quiet moments were over, we went about our business at the Smithsonian. After the visit, the Elders saw a "news guy," as they called him, in our hotel lobby and hurried up to tell him their story. That reporter, Peter Mansbridge, listened, and then put them on the flagship CBC-TV news program *The National* a few days later.[96] These days when I travel, I try to remember to do as the Elders did—to visit nearby water, to remember the importance of sintering, joining, coalescing, and to remember that wherever I am, I am attached to the land and the waters. I take a moment to quiet and calm and think about how I'm coming to someone else's home with responsibilities, and that this is an opportunity to iterate and bond.

Where I live now, I recognize that the headwaters of the Mississippi River act as the western doorway of the Anishinaabeg nation. I can see our language, anglicized, in the river's name—*misi* meaning big, and *sippi* or *ziibi* meaning river. According to The Decolonial Atlas, there are six Anishinaabe names for the Mississippi, from Lake Itasca into the Gulf of Mexico:

Omashkoozo-ziibi (Elk River)—the Mississippi
    River between Lake Itasca and Lake Bemidji

Bemijigamaag-ziibi (Traversing Lake's River)—
    the Mississippi River between Lake Bemidji
    and Cass Lake

Gaa-miskwaawaakokaag-ziibi (River abundant
    with Red Cedar)—the Mississippi River
    between Cass Lake and Lake Winnibigoshish

Wiinibiigoonzhish-ziibi (Little Stagnant Murky
    River)—the Mississippi River between Lake
    Winnibigoshish and the Leech Lake River

Gichi-ziibi (Big River)—the Mississippi River
    between the Leech Lake River and the Crow
    Wing River

Misi-ziibi (Great River)—the Mississippi River
    between the Crow Wing River and the
    Gulf of Mexico.[97]

I know enough to understand that this list is partial, just
a start, and that local Anishinaabeg and other Indigenous
peoples belonging to the river would have had, and still
have, hundreds of names for specific places along the river.

To me, the big river feels like a very distant relative—one I
don't know. One to whom I am related, although I'm not sure
exactly how. When I hear the name *Gichi-ziibi*, I think of the
St. Lawrence River, not the Mississippi—although I know this
will only be true for me and others who are eastern Nishnaabeg.

The other thing I think about is a poem by Lucille Clifton:

the mississippi river empties into the gulf
and the gulf enters the sea and so forth,
none of them emptying anything,
all of them carrying yesterday
forever on their white tipped backs,
all of them dragging forward tomorrow
it is the great circulation
of the earth's body, like the blood

of the gods, this river in which the past
is always flowing. every water
is the same water coming around.
everyday someone is standing on the edge
of this river, staring into time,
whispering mistakenly:
only here, only now.[98]

Last year I flew to New Orleans for a panel at the American Studies Association's annual meeting, and I wrote that poem in my journal to carry with me. I loved "none of them emptying anything" followed by the reminder "all of them carrying yesterday."

The other book I carried with me on that trip is William C. Anderson's *The Nation on No Map: Black Anarchism and Abolition*. I had been rereading it because William was also on the panel in New Orleans, the city sitting beside the big river. I was sintering with Gchi Ziibing, Lucille Clifton, William C. Anderson, Black Anarchism and Black Feminism.[99]

I brought cattails and water lilies and bullfrogs with me, and I asked myself, What can those engaged in forms of Indigenous struggle learn from those engaged in forms of Black struggle? What can I learn, as I sit here on the turtle's back and choose not to build a Westphalian state, from others engaged in struggle and world building that refuses the same containers as I do?

In his book, Anderson asks us to consider a vision of politics that "no longer has the state as its object or horizon and eschews the calcified forms of politics as usual . . . where the state is no longer the horizon of possibility or the telos of struggle."[100]

This is a relief to read, even as it also marks a lonely path. This vision of politics means no more apologies, no more Royal Commissions and National Inquiries, no more Assembly of First Nations, Indian Act, Self-Government Agreements, Rights, Court—no more, no more, no more. No more begging neoliberalism for recognition. No more begging for charges and convictions. No more being bound up in the cyclical terror of never-ending court cases, negotiations and research projects so tightly controlled that the predetermined outcomes include pacifying resistance. It is a relief, and it also places me on a different trajectory from many others engaged in Indigenous struggle. I don't mean to fault those who have tried and continue to try to make life and living better for First Nations people and our communities, and I don't mean to diminish the gains they have made with issues such as clean drinking water or housing, for example. But I do mean that we must study and examine our strategies. And I do mean to bask, even if briefly, in the flight path opened by changing the horizon.

What might it mean for our view to be transformed towards liberation? So much Indigenous activism, organizing, research and writing focuses on the state: the rights the state bestows upon us and then whittles away, the promises the state has made to us, and the legal architecture of Indigenous–state relations—holding it accountable, appealing to it and demanding our recognition within it. The state is built on our backs, with our lands and with the nested ecologies of the non-human persons within which we exist. There is a legal and political apparatus around this exploitation and genocide, an apparatus that ties Indigenous peoples to the state for the state's purposes. The apparatus includes the

Indian Act, treaties, land claim settlements, comprehensive and specific claims processes, the legal system, Aboriginal Rights, Aboriginal Title, the Constitution—and I can go on and on. This entanglement with the state, while it may be necessary for us as a practice of survival, imagines state formation as the ideal vessel, and therefore limits our visions of the future, limits how we see our own formations, our nation-hoods and our collective arrangements within, or around, the nation-state. As Anderson states in the first chapter of his book, it benefits the state and our oppressors for us to remain invested in the story of reforming that state rather than abolishing it.[101]

The thinker Saidiya Hartman writes movingly that Black people have been relegated to live outside the state and its social contract. For centuries, they have been abandoned by the state, not embraced within it as persons or citizens. They have lived inside the nation-state as external alien, as resource to be extracted, as property, as disposable population.[102]

For centuries, Indigenous peoples have built societies in formations that are anti-state, with a social contract that isn't a contract at all but an ecology of caretaking. Nation-states were built on top of us, using our bodies, minds, spirits and land as resources and materials, or as threats to state sovereignty that were targeted for elimination. Our relationality was considered extractable and disposable. At the same time, since the arrival of the white man, we have also engaged in anarchistic resistances, without necessarily laying claim to anarchism as a politics.

Now, with his words, William C. Anderson invites me, invites us, to spend some time thinking alongside and learning from Black anarchy. I am reading his work for ideas of

what might lie beyond the nation-state, for ways of organizing we haven't yet tried, for analysis that leads to radical
planetary visions and ways of relating that allow for and
nourish Anishinaabeg bimaadiziwin, that unfold as Indigenous resistance, as resurgence, as decolonial feminisms.

Anderson models a beautiful practice of dabaadendiz-
iwin, or humility, in his acknowledgements. He asks us to
give his project, his book, his thinking and his writing a
chance. Quoting Aimé Césaire's resignation from the French
Communist Party, he takes up Césaire's call to use Marxism
and Communism in the service of Black people, not Black
peoples in the service of Marxism and Communism.[103]

Anderson writes, "We should avoid service to ideology
and let all that we can gather from different ideas work in
service to us."[104]

This seems like a simple directive. It seems like something that already should be common practice for those of
us engaged in various forms of struggle. But I know it is
more difficult to enact than it might appear. I think it may
be an imperative that is clear to hunters, trappers and fishers, for instance, but is perhaps lost or harder to hold on
to in the city, in the academy and in organizing circles.
As I return home, I keep it in my thoughts as a directive
to carry through the writing of my own book, and in my
practice of bimaadiziwin and Nishnaabeg intercommunalism. Maybe, I think, I don't need to reclaim "feminism";
maybe I simply need to read about and practise it in a decolonial Nishnaabeg way, one that is in service to the liberation of living beings.[105]

Gizhewaadiziwin

Gizhewaadiziwin is unconditional love and kindness in a daily practice of mutual aid. And these days, it is something I think about and try to embody continually. During the wildfire season of 2023, when the capital city of Yellowknife was evacuated, its inhabitants were sent to a place eighteen hours' drive south because of out-of-control and unprecedented wildfires threatening the community. As I watched my Dene friends and colleagues quickly organize themselves against the backdrop of colonial inequality, I saw many embodying their Dene Laws, sintering practices that in times of crisis and panic guide individuals and communities towards care, kindness and unconditional love. This care took many forms: Sitting with Elders and convincing them to get on a plane and evacuate. Driving family members south. Making sure old ones had their prescriptions, clean laundry, food and places to stay. Helping parents with child care. Taking care of pets left behind. I started rereading Dean Spade's book *Mutual Aid: Building Solidarity During This Crisis* (and, I would add, the next) as I witnessed Dene mutual aid coming to life in the face of wildfire, and here it acts as a companion in my exploration of Gizhewaadiziwin.

In my life, Doug is the person who embodied this practice of mutual aid most consistently, although of course
he wasn't the only one who did so. He was my example,
though, and I saw that, as he practised sintering, he also
practised reciprocity: the idea that we Nishnaabeg give of
ourselves, or we give offerings or gifts, in exchange for taking the time, labour, presence or—in the case of harvesting
plants and animals—lives of others. I understood through
him that reciprocity is more complicated than simply an
exchange that mutually benefits individuals. Reciprocity
must be systemic. Scale is important. While reciprocity does
indeed take place between individuals, families, communities
and nations, it also attends to a relationality beyond the two
individuals or entities involved. Within the network it is
understood that when we are working well together and in
balance, the needs of all living things will be met. When one
engages in an individual act of reciprocity, one is feeding
the network.

Reciprocity is not an exchange of money for goods and
services, nor is it an exchange of ownership or property. It is
an investment in a system of care that extends beyond one's
individuality. And an individual act of reciprocity does not
necessarily result in an immediate reward. Harvesters, for
instance, distribute food to the community for their entire
lives, and may or may not ever be in a situation where they
cannot harvest for themselves and need that care. However,
it is possible that one of the recipients of a harvester's food,
or perhaps a family member of that recipient, might make
something out of a hide the harvester had gifted them.
A recipient might share a story with the harvester, and they
might not. Our system of care is complex, and it is never

transactional. It is a practice, and when living beings engage in this practice, everyone is eventually cared for.

For Nishnaabeg, the way we live makes the world.

Anishinaabe scholars Aaron Mills and Niigaan Sinclair refer to the practice of gift giving or making offerings as bagijiganan. They both write, in slightly different ways, that this practice is one of the most important social, political and ideological interactions for co-creating Anishinaabeg life—or, to put it another way, for the maintenance of mino-bimaadiziwin.[106] Similarly, Anishinaabeg biologist Robin Wall Kimmerer writes, in the book *Braiding Sweetgrass*, of miinigowizin: the idea that the Anishinaabeg live in a world made of gifts.[107] Miinigowizin is not capital, it is not a transaction, nor is it gifts of property. It is a practice of sintering, and a practice of strengthening or forming bonds. The gifts themselves don't matter. It is the process around the gift, a sharing of belongings, that drives the system.

One of the first times I saw this in motion, I was in my early twenties. I was with an Elder and we were hunting for geese in northern Ontario. Once we got to the spot where we would hunt, he told me that he didn't carry tobacco because it was expensive, and he didn't smoke. The only thing he had with him was his snack—a bologna sandwich. He broke off a small piece of the sandwich and offered it to the geese, along with prayer—not the sort of prayer he'd learned in residential school or the church, but a more intimate conversation between his spirit and the spirit of the geese. We didn't shoot any geese that day because none came close enough. On our way home in the truck, I asked if we hadn't shot any geese because our offering was bologna not tobacco. The Elder thought, smiled at my naïveté, and explained that the spirits were loving and kind, and would know that all he had was a bologna sandwich, and see that it was a very nice thing to share with them. Bologna, he taught me, is just as good as tobacco if it is honest and offered with an open heart.

That day, and many days since, I've made offerings and given gifts without "getting" anything immediately in return. Yet on that day I did receive many gifts—teachings and practices from the Elder, his time, care and presence, and a visit with the geese where they disrupted capitalist systems of exchange and taught me that they were not food in the sky but a sovereign nation of beings with whom we co-create the world. And here I am, more than twenty years later, reflecting on the time we spent together, learning.

All these teachings are expressions of a spiritual and physical world-building practice grounded in the belief that every living thing with a spirit also has a gift to share with the community, and a responsibility to find that gift and use it to bring forth more life. We continually ask ourselves: What can I give, or give up, to promote more life? When we see someone in need, we ask: What can I give to this person to make their life even a little bit better? Gifting, sharing, giftways, giveaways, the redistribution of gifts, the divestment of one's gifts for the betterment of another— all these are ways of making the world.

This practice also fits within the larger concept of mino-bimaadiziwin—life in relation, with the purpose of bringing forth more life; and with the overarching concept of Gizhewaadiziwin—living lives of generosity, benevolence, love (in the sense of connection and attachment to other living beings), kindness, compassion for all, sharing, caring, respect, humility and tenderness.[108]

Mutual aid is a foundational world-building process of Nishinaabeg life, and it is easy to find examples of how it manifests in our daily practices. An infant might first encounter mutual aid through breastfeeding, the nurturing of attachment between parent and child through the sharing of sustenance, connection and warmth. A toddler, marching around, expressing in a true, unfiltered way every emotion they might be feeling, brings humour and insight and connection to the family. A teenager engaged in the fast life, pushing boundaries, swimming in consequences, teaches us about different sorts of freedom. In adulthood, storytellers become conduits of knowledge as they share narratives—vessels of imagination, thought, collaboration and co-creation.[109] And ceremonies enact healing, peace and intimacy. Hunters gift meat and fish; harvesters gift rice, maple sugar, berries and medicines; grandparents gift child care; Elders gift presence and experience. Artists gift possibilities beyond our current structures. Singers and drummers gift prayers.

I think of mutual aid when I recall Mohawk women gathering around kitchen tables, organizing to stop golf course expansions, condominium development, enclosures around nature areas. Or when I remember the women of Grassy Narrows organizing to protect their lands and bodies from clear-cutting and toxic contamination. Or Two-Spirit, queer and trans young people researching, writing and distributing their work in *You Are Made of Medicine: A Mental Health Peer Support Manual for Indigiqueer, Two-Spirit, LGBTQ+, and Gender Non-conforming Indigenous Youth*.[110] Or the Braided Warriors, organizing a temporary blockade

of Indigenous youth in March 2020 in unceded territories of
the Səl̓ilwətaʔ (Tsleil-Waututh), Sḵwx̱wú7mesh (Squamish)
and xʷməθkʷəy̓əm (Musqueam) nations, and demanding
the release of an Elder jailed for participation in protests
against the Trans Mountain pipeline in Burnaby, BC.[111] Or
the Tiny House Warriors protecting Secwépemc lands from
the same pipeline. Or the Unist'ot'en camp. #LandBack
and 1492 Land Back Lane. And I could go on, recalling and
naming blockades as generative refusals of the state—generative precisely because, behind the barricades, collectives
are rebuilding their own versions of Gizhewaadiziwin. They
are building worlds outside the ones we have inherited.[112]
I'm thinking, too, of the student encampments for Gaza that
blossomed in the spring of 2024, and the communities that
supported them in myriad ways, from decision-making to
cooking to child care to teach-ins to a solidarity that centred the voices of Gazans. I'm thinking of the slogan "we
keep us safe," and abolitionist practices put into practice,
because of course university administrations and the police
were threatening violence.

In other words: behind the barricades, whether those
blockades are enacted on Anishinaabeg land at Grassy Narrows, Dakota land at Standing Rock, at the port of Vancouver
or at Unist'ot'en, blockades are rich sites of Indigenous life.

In the spaces behind the barricades, you'll find parents
with children. You'll find Elders. You'll encounter ceremony,
sacred fires and language learning. Art making. Singing.
Drumming. Storytelling.

You'll find an ethic of care and mutual aid as harvesters
and cooks engage in a bush economy to feed the front lines
alongside spiritual leaders, nurses and medics taking care of

the people. You will notice a mobilized network of support and solidarity extending well beyond the barricades.

You will witness the re-emergence of political leaders, not through a band council election but through Indigenous practices of deep relationality.

You will enter a collective embodiment of Indigenous legal practices.

You will hear sounds of political, intellectual and spiritual engagement in these rich sites of knowledge production, and you'll see Indigenous anti-colonial theory generated in real time, through embodied collective practice.

In spite of dominant colonialism—in the face of it—you will witness a radically different political existence and ethical orientation. This existence, and this orientation, springs from a different premise than the politics and economy of extraction. The premise is to live with the purpose of generating continual life.[113]

You will see us living the way Nibi did, in the moments before they decided to flood.

16

Flowing

Doug had mixed feelings about the amount of time I spent in the north, with Dene Elders, over the last decade. On one hand, he saw me grow, taking our Anishinaabeg concepts and philosophies and pulling them into conversation with the Elders and their thinking. He saw me learn skills like making dry fish and fishing with nets that are far more difficult to find in our part of the world. He loved looking at the photos on my phone of huge trout, large tracts of undisturbed lands and cold winters. For him, it was like looking back to the time of his grandparents and great-grandparents. On the other hand, I know he wished I was doing this work at home, with our people. I also know he wanted to come with me, but by the time that could have been possible, he was on dialysis and travel was an ordeal. Instead, he visited the north through the stories I told him from the passenger seat of his truck as we drove around and visited the frogs, wolves and lakes in our territory.

If he were alive now, I'd be asking him about enawendi-win—the spiritual and material relations or strands that connect all parts of Creation; and waawiyeyaag—the interwoven systems that combine to create nindinawemaganidog, or all our relations, or the great family of living relationships that make up everything Anishinaabeg. I'd ask him about these concepts because I've been reading about them,[114] and I wish I could know how they resonated with him and his understanding of the world. I certainly see our people practising these concepts, but I wonder if he knew the words themselves, and if they entered his own thinking. I'm interested because they seem to me to describe the material and spiritual forces that bind Nishnaabeg into the network of life; and they seem to describe the very process of sintering, or belonging, that I've been exploring in life and in these words—that continual practice of relating to all the living things with which one shares time and space within a homeland, and on planet earth.

In the summer of 2017, I spent time in the north again, in Kaska Dena territory, with Elders from Tū Łídīini, or Ross River, and in the mountains of Dechin la', in the shared territory of the Kaska Dena and Shútah Dene. Dechin la' is located in what is known in the Shútahot'íne language as Nío Nę P'énę, meaning the backbone of the animals who travel here, the backbone of the world. While living on the spine of the world, I learned about Dena ā́ nézen, a concept and practice that is like enawendiwin. I wished I had brought Doug here, to talk with these Elders about these concepts.

I was with my friend and co-worker Josh Barichello, a kuskāni or white person, who has spent many years living and learning with Kaska Dena Elders. I was helping him with his MA thesis research, and he was helping me think through, *feel through* and articulate the ways Indigenous peoples make worlds through sintering and fostering deep relationality. On a long drive from the airstrip at Mile 222 to the camp at Dechin la', he explained to me that the term *Dena* was typically translated as "person," reflecting the close tie between Dena and the land. *Dena* is a word that encompasses many beings. He explained that *Mesgâ Dena* meant Raven People, *Gēs Dena* meant Salmon People, and *Sōn Dena* meant Star People. These animals were, in English terminology, "peoples" within Kaska Dena, though with their own ways of governing and their own body of knowledge that they brought to Dena society.

This made complete sense to me, and I see similarities to Michi Saagiig Nishnaabeg thought: There is no hierarchy to Creation. Humans are not exceptional. What happens, I wondered, when we extend the Eurocentric conceptualization of "human" to animals and plants and rivers? What happens when we understand Nibi as Water People?

Josh had learned much from Kaska Dena Elders. He told me *Dena* means something like "flowing from land," as *de* means flow or flowing and *ne* is a way of saying land. The word *Á'* comes from *Á'íi*, a term embedded with power and a special level of respect. He reminded me that the teachings of Á'íi were embodied daily by the Elders of Tū Łídīini as they walked through the world. Some beings or places, he said, can be Á'íi. Special places on the land, such as mineral licks, are associated with unique codes that prohibit people from camping too close to them or making loud noises in their vicinity because of the Á'íi that surrounds them. Human actions that will result in negative consequences can be Á'íi. When people become too greedy and don't embody the Dena principle of sharing, they might have bad luck because it is Á'íi to behave in this way. Similarly, it is Á'íi to step over important tools like guns and fishnets, and if this happens, the hunters and fishers using these tools might have bad luck with their harvest. Animals with special powers, and who therefore must be treated extra carefully, can be Á'íi. For example, because of their Á'íi, Tēzūne (river otters) must be skinned and cleaned in the bush, away from villages or camps. Witnessing certain phenomena associated with A'ii, phenomena that are considered omens, can be dangerous.

Living according to Á'íi instills people with a profound sense of respect for themselves, for one another and for the world around them. Á'íi is a constant reminder of the implications that your actions will have. It emphasizes the need to think about how your actions will affect others, to be conscious of the collective, to walk with empathy.

Nézen is another important word in Dena that Josh explained to me. It is a third-person conjugation of the verbs "to think" and "to feel," but is also much more than either the English verbs *thinking* or *feeling* on their own. Rather, it is thinking and feeling at once, or a sintering of them together. Kaska Dena Elders will often say that when speaking in English, you are speaking through your head, but when speaking in Kaska Dena, you are speaking through your heart.[115]

Flowing
Thinking
Feeling
Sintering

It is through Dena ā́ nézen that the Kaska Dena govern their relations with living beings in their territory. This includes a strong responsibility to share, a deep respect for land and all the beings that are part of it, and a system of consent, thanksgiving and care that ensures all the communities that make up the Kaska Dena world continue to exist and remain healthy and well for the coming generations. Dena a̓ nézen affirms the autonomy of living things such as caribou, who are considered thinking, spiritual and emotional beings, full actors in world making. According to Elders Norman Sterriah and Mary Maja, this means that the people must stay away from calving grounds and salt licks. It means taking only what one needs and sharing the harvest with everyone. It means stopping the harvest when animal communities are struggling—or, as Norm said, when an area is "skinny on caribou"—and waiting until they recover before hunting again. It means living in a way that respects the life cycles, movement, knowledge, land use and autonomy of these animals.

Such an approach is in sharp contrast to Western resource management regimes, which focus on counting and controlling animal populations as if they are resources that exist for the benefit of humans, whether that "benefit" is mining, capitalism-fuelled climate change or non-Indigenous hunting adventures in Kaska Dena country.[116]

These days, thinking about my conversations in different places and times with both Josh and Doug, I wonder about the potential of Indigenous intercommunalism. Such exchanges were so foundational in our past histories, and more recently were key to how both Doug, on our land in the south, and the Elders from Tū Łídīini, in the north, made the world. I wonder if we could recalibrate our organizing and turn away from reforming the state's relation-

ship to Indigenous peoples towards work that meets the
needs of living beings on a local and planetary scale. Could
this be a mechanism for enacting a Nishinaabeg rubric of
care, reducing the reliance of our peoples on the state while
increasing our own self-reliance—as well as our reliance on
networks of care with other oppressed peoples? Such a shift
would reduce our collective political efforts to reform the
state and, as Miriame Kaba says, bolster possibility beyond the
state. Could such a practice, communally embodied, generate
the dreams, visions, skills and knowledge for world building towards liberation? These "survival tactics" could turn
us away from begging the state for resources, recognition,
reconciliation, environmental protection and just relations,
and place our bodies, minds and spirits in the position to
make a different present.

I am often struck by how survival tactics look different
outside cities and urban centres. I think, on the one hand,
of the Dene fishers who distribute their catch to Elders in
their rural community. On the other hand, I think of a vol-
unteer-run initiative in the city of Winnipeg, an initiative
called Ikwe Safe Ride, created by seven community women
(Heather, Dana, Lacey, Charlotte, Violet, Chery and Chris-
tine) to provide a safe alternative to taxis for Indigenous
women and children.[117] In both cases, care and survival go
together, are generated by the community and exist outside
the system of the state.

I think, too, about Tū Łídīini Elder Charlie Dick, whose
voice Josh quotes in his work. Dick articulated for Josh the
Dena idea that land cannot be owned or bought or sold or
traded, because it is not property. Land cannot be divided
and managed by arbitrary lines on a map.[118] To Dick, the

word *land* is a shorthand for the Dena's relationships with plants, animals, humans, ancestors, future generations, spiritual beings and all life in the place they live. But, as Josh has noted, Kaska Dena hunters have recently witnessed a sharp decline in the communities of animals with whom they share land. They point to climate change, habitat loss from resource extraction, and unsustainable hunting practices that leave the caribou herds struggling.

Other, poignant stories Josh recounts in his thesis reinforce this change. In one, he travels with a Dena Elder named Amos, who grew up before roads, crossing the land by dog team and the rivers in a moose-skin boat. As the two of them arrive at a shore Amos and his family have been visiting for over ninety years, they find settlers camped on the site, and the Elder's energy abruptly shifts. Beer cans, pickup trucks and eight moose are strewn around the camp. No one acknowledges Amos, and after a few minutes he suggests to Josh, with pain in his eyes, that the two of them leave and return home.[119]

When I read this passage in Josh's thesis, I thought about how I'd seen a similar look of pain in Doug's face a hundred times. It happened most often when we were paddling in our lakes and he would take me to an island to show me something—a place where he used to camp or where his grandmother picked cranberries—only to find a brand new monster home in the spot where he used to live on the land. Or only to find settlers not only occupying but destroying the network of living things that were originally there. Destroying history, yes—but also destroying the present, and the potential for Nishnaabeg futures.

And yet this is precisely why I believe the concept of Indigenous intercommunalism holds out such hope. It was painful experiences such as Doug's and Amos's that led the Ross River Dena Council and the Ross River Elders Council to continue to organize to protect their homeland. They not only refused colonial management of their own bodies and community, they also refused the colonial resource management of their living relations. Seeing the imposition of whiteness and the colonial system of "resource management" causing harm to the Kaska Dena network of life, they took on the management and responsibility themselves. Now it is not only the Kaska Dena who are following Dena a᷃ nézen. It applies to all humans who take from the land, and the Ross River Dena Council and Ross River Elders Council came up with their own permit system for non–Kaska Dena hunters. They closed certain areas to harvesting, based on their knowledge of animal populations. And they require all hunters to follow Dena a᷃ nézen, ensuring the health and well-being of caribou, moose, bighorn sheep, Dena and all living things in these ecosystems.

This is deep caretaking—a mutual aid that extends beyond humans, and a restoration of everything flowing from the land.

Aabijijiwan, Continual Flowing

What you do every day makes you who you are.

Maddy Whetung, in her thesis "At the Shore," writes about growing up in the 1990s with a grandfather, Clifford Whetung, who taught her the everyday joy of living together with accountability, care, rest and reciprocity. He did this often through work in his large garden, gathering whoever was around and giving them little jobs to do in the garden while he went about his daily tasks. He paid each of the children a small hourly wage and relied upon them to report their hours. He gave few instructions and did not hover over his grandchildren, trusting them to figure things out and ask questions if needed. He never got angry or frustrated or raised his voice. He placed a profound level of trust in each child, and Maddy remembers striving to meet that trust with good work. All the grandchildren worked in the garden, regardless of gender or ability, and he met each one with the same presence and kindness. And on their way home from the garden, after a day of steady work and an afternoon rest, Clifford Whetung would deliver bags of vegetables to different homes in the community.

It was this everydayness, the repeated practice of being with her grandfather in his garden during the long days of summer, that reinforced for Maddy the Michi Saagiig Nishnaabeg idea that you are what you do, and that what you do every day matters because over time this accumulates into the structure of one's life and the structure of a community's life. Growing vegetables and sharing them with the community isn't a groundbreaking activity. Yet, from a Nishnaabeg perspective, doing this every summer, year after year, becomes an opportunity to model, teach and embody the Kokum Dibaajimowin repeatedly.[120]

Hearing this story from Maddy reinforces for me that how you flow (or not) through life is both emergent and defining.

The never-ending flow of the global water cycle reciprocally nourishes life on the planet and teaches us about accountability. When part of the cycle is disrupted, modes of reciprocity are disrupted, and the everyday cycle of accountability is disturbed.

What happens when the accountability system is interrupted? Recently, I've been rereading and thinking with Olúfẹ́mi O. Táíwò's *Elite Capture: How the Powerful Took Over Identity Politics (and Everything Else)*. In my reading this time, I'm thinking not so much about identity politics but about what's in parentheses—the "everything else." Táíwò defines "elite capture" as "a concept that originated in developing countries to describe the way socially advantaged people tend to gain control over financial benefits, specifically foreign aid, meant for others." And the concept, he writes, "has also been applied more generally to describe how political projects can be hijacked in principle or effect by the well positioned and resourced."[121]

In response to this, I'm thinking about how Indigenous political projects are hijacked in principle and in effect by the Canadian state, and how over time Indigenous political projects become more responsive to the ruling class, or elites, or the state than they are to Indigenous communities. (I'm also thinking I'm old—since I used to understand this concept not as "elite capture" but as hegemony[122]—even as I admire the brilliance, clarity and power of Táíwò's thinking.)

From an Indigenous perspective—and certainly from within the Michi Saagiig Nishnaabeg perspective, which I would characterize as radically egalitarian—"elite capture" arrived through colonialism. It is a tool of the system of colonialism, one that became prominent after the Indian Act amendments of 1951, when Indigenous peoples started to organize in ways that made our struggles more visible to the outside. For one thing, we were then allowed to gather our resources, and hire lawyers, and organize in ways that had not been available to us in the past. Over the past forty years in Canada, the idea of Indigenous self-determination has yielded an unprecedented degree of recognition for Aboriginal and Treaty Rights within the apparatus of the state, including through the Constitution Act of 1982. At the same time, anti-imperialist traditions have been used to refute the idea that the relationship between Indigenous peoples and the state can be transformed by the politics of recognition. As Glen Coulthard argues, drawing on Frantz Fanon, the terms of recognition in Canada are determined solely by the state, and while the politics of recognition have replaced the state's more overt policy of assimilation, the state is still trying to extinguish and eliminate Indigenous Title and power, and to control land and capital.[123]

But now it strikes me, reading Táíwò, that Indigenous political projects, framed in the politics of recognition, have set up our rebellions and revolts for elite capture.

This pattern of recognition politics followed by elite capture plays out over and over for Indigenous peoples. For example, the political project of reparations for the destruction caused by residential schools—through recognition of individual harms, court-defined justice, payouts, veneered apologies, and the Truth and Reconciliation Commission—has, according to the Yellowhead Institute's 2022 Status Update on Reconciliation, resulted in thirteen out of ninety-four recommendations completed, seven years after those recommendations were made.[124] Similarly, the political project of building a society where both the acronym MMIWG2S and the reality it describes are unthinkable was similarly transformed into an inquiry that resulted in a similar report with even less progress. The long years of work and struggle for self-determination by survivors of residential schools and families of the disappeared were captured by the state, used to make that state look benevolent and just, and furthermore co-opted to quell Indigenous protest. Elites within the state could then continue to invest in it with certainty.

Elite capture ensures that despite forty years of political projects focused on Indigenous self-determination, land rights and our ability to make decisions in our homelands for our peoples, we have less land than before, and we are enmeshed in a comprehensive land claims process that refuses self-determination as a necessary condition for being involved in the negotiating process at all.

Of course, many Indigenous organizers see this and reject the politics of recognition. Recent examples of such resistance include the Unist'ot'en camp, the 1492 Land Back Lane and the Tiny House Warriors. It takes vision and a moral commitment beyond our present moment to resist in this way. It takes a belief in mino-bimaadiziwin—and it takes embodying that belief in one's actions. It takes flow, an everyday practice of accountability and reciprocity, to ensure that our movements and acts of resistance aren't captured and rendered inert. And if they are captured, Nibi directs us to find a way to leak, escape and wear down the container, and once again restore flow.

For me, a galvanizing Anishinaabe example of this sort of resistance is the Slant Lake blockade in the homeland of Grassy Narrows First Nation.

Sixteen years ago, I took my mom and two small children on a trip to northern Ontario, to the communities of Wabauskang and Grassy Narrows. The trip took a lot of effort. In the first stage, four of us were cramped into three airplane seats with busy bags, my mom's purse full of snacks in twist-tied baggies, and me with a tiny, crappy CD player and ten discs full of Thomas the Tank Engine. When our plane landed in Thunder Bay, nearly eight hours after we'd left the house, we were only halfway there. We still had a six-hour drive ahead of us—the kids in their car seats, asking to stop for a break every twenty minutes.

But it was an important trip to make. The people in the communities of Wabauskang and Grassy Narrows had been dealing for years with the effects of the contamination of their waterway. I think about them now, years later, as I write these words and try to understand what happens when water is weaponized—when its power is captured by elites and turned against mino-bimaadiziwin, whether that is happening in Gaza or the West Bank or in Grassy Narrows.

And I remember the words of David Suzuki when he spoke in 2018 at Toronto Metropolitan University during an event leading up to Grassy Narrows's annual River Run action. In tears, his voice wavering, he said, "My inspiration comes from the fact that you haven't given up."[125]

Therein lies one of the foundational teachings Grassy Narrows has gifted us: be like Nibi.

An unwavering commitment to caring for their families and the network of life embedded in Anishinaabek worlds has, for decades, carried the Grassy Narrows community through broken treaty relations, relocation, the impacts of hydroelectric development, residential schools and child welfare practices, and of course the eliminating violence of pollution. Starting in 1913 and continuing to the present day, the pulp and paper industry in the municipalities of Dryden and Kenora has dumped an array of toxic substances into the river, including an infamous ten metric tons of untreated mercury in the 1960s and 1970s, and more recently bleaching waste that produces phenols, polychlorinated dibenzodioxins (PCDDs) and polychlorinated dibenzofurans (PCDFs), also known as dioxins and furans. Still, even this is only part of the story. To make pulp, one needs trees—trees who share their time and space with bears and moose, blueberries and Labrador tea. Trees lived with the Anishinaabek long before their worth, our worth, was measured in dollars.

On that visit sixteen years ago, Judy DaSilva drove me out to the Slant Lake blockade in Grassy Narrows. The blockade had started as a flashpoint a few years earlier. On December 2, 2002, after more than a decade of letter writing, meetings, protests, petitions, speaking tours and legal efforts to protect their homeland from further industrial development without their consent, young Anishinaabek had lain down on the logging road to prevent large multinational corporations from destroying traplines, hunting grounds, berry patches, medicines, and plant and animal habitats in order to supply mills in Dryden and Kenora with trees. And while the companies Abitibi and Weyerhaeuser continued to log the more remote sections of Grassy Narrows's territory, in the summer of 2008 AbitibiBowater was finally forced to give up their licence to the Whiskey Jack Forest and commit to no logging without consent from the community. This halted all logging on Grassy Narrows's territory.

It was a tremendous victory—but also a fragile one. Today, despite the Ontario provincial government's 2018 land declaration that banned all mineral staking, exploration, mining and logging in the territory, that government under Premier Doug Ford is now proposing to open part of Grassy Narrows's territory to industrial logging in their upcoming management plan. And despite the land declaration, the Ontario government has also allowed mineral claims by mining companies and prospectors to grow into the thousands even as they grant drilling permits to a few companies.

When water is weaponized, Grassy Narrows teaches us to be like Nibi: to stick with our purpose in the face of disaster, to fight back, to flow and persist, to flood or scale up our visions for a better world. It also teaches us to sinter: to develop relationships with other resistors—Palestinians, the Wet'suwet'en, Kayapo and Ovaherero, and Black feminist abolitionists—dreaming worlds beyond this present one.

I think of those precious Anishinaabeg who put words into action two decades ago in Grassy Narrows, and did what they had to do to pass their homeland to the next generation with as much sanctity as possible. I'm so grateful for their challenge to me, and all of us, to see beyond our scaled-down, state-sanctioned visions of a better world, and to remake the worlds of our ancestors, where forests and rivers are our precious relatives.[126]

When my friend Judy DaSilva, now an Elder, and I sat at the blockade that day sixteen years ago, it was quiet—nothing at all like the photographs I'd seen of this place at the height of the protest: arms blocking logging trucks, hand drumming, children, feast food and sacred fires. But here it was, and here we were. I'd known Judy for a very long time, and as always, I found her energy striking—calm and grounded, the very best of all the Seven Ancestor teachings wrapped into a person who lived a big kindness, kino-bimaadiziwin. I thought of the map of these sites which had held similar mobilizations to protect land—Anicinaabe Park, Kanehsatà:ke, Ipperwash, Burnt Church, Denendeh and Lyle Island, to start—as beaver dams, blocking logging trucks and golf courses, refusing the life of capital on one hand, and regenerating the political and social structures of the people on the other. I thought of the sinter that had taken place behind the barricades, and the worlds sintering gives birth to.

Recapturing

Over our twenty-year friendship, I often asked Doug about water. But he mostly refused to talk to me about it because in our culture, water is the responsibility of women. When we were teaching together, he would often invite Shirley Williams to speak to the class about water, and he was careful not to interfere with what she told us. Shirley is an Odawa Elder and a gifted language expert. She would often tell the story of travelling on the lake as a child with her dad, who warned her that the water was becoming polluted. He cautioned her that eventually she might have to buy water.[127] I will always remember the look on her face when she got to this part of the story: a mixture of shock and horror that something her dad told her nearly eighty years ago, and that had sounded unbelievable at the time, had come true.

Today, what I'm learning from water is that when Nibi is captured, Nibi adapts and stays the course.

Twenty years of the Slant Lake blockade demonstrates to me that Indigenous Knowledge systems hold the potential to not only critique capitalism but reveal multiple potentials to live otherwise.[128] These systems provided my ancestors with the moral and ethical imperatives to critique, analyze and revolt. I'm here today, in no small part, because of how my ancestors acted and lived within those moral imperatives. This teaches me that we don't need to rely solely on anti-imperialist and anti-colonial traditions to critique our present moment; we also can draw upon our own intimate anti-colonial tradition, one that is at once theory and communal embodied practice. Our contribution internationally to anti-colonialism comes from these bodies of knowledge. I feel the need to articulate these knowledge systems because I think they can help build worlds that are otherwise, and because I believe in the value of sintering: sharing our knowledge with, and as, anti-colonial peoples helps us and helps our collective movements.

I believe there must be a shift away from making Indigenous Knowledge knowable, legible and shareable by the state and its actors; instead, we must refocus this knowledge towards liberation. Just because Nishnaabeg worlds are deeply relational does not mean we should be in relationship with everyone, and it especially doesn't mean we should be in relationship with all the forces that attack mino-bimaadiziwin. Quite the opposite. The deeply relational nature of our worlds means that we must fight against systems that attack and undermine the planetary network of life.

Indigenous Knowledge is regularly captured by elites—some working in the academy, some working for state bureaucracies—who separate our knowledge from our bodies, from our peoples and from political projects and, too often now, deploy it in the service of neoliberalism. Looking back at all my writing, I can see that this is something I've been writing about all along, since I began my PhD research years ago, using different framings to respond to different colonial interventions over the last few decades.

Institutions such as universities and the agencies that fund research were for decades, and still are, only just beginning to acknowledge Indigenous Knowledge, and only ever on their terms. The recognition of Indigenous Knowledge was and is being driven by the state, non-Indigenous researchers and even environmental activists who see our bodies of knowledge as enhancements to Western science and Western natural resource management strategies. Our knowledge is seen, on the one hand, as a potential source of solutions for pending environmental issues such as climate change, and on the other hand as a way of placating Indigenous peoples' resistance and objections to industrial development by making us feel included, consulted, part of environmental impact assessments, and stakeholders in decision-making. This is, at best, a partial recognition, a partial seeing: the state and the academy are interested in information in English, and in documented data rather than ethics and philosophies. Knowledge Holders are often interviewed, and then these interviews are transcribed into English, extracting the knowledge from the Oral Tradition and Indigenous languages. Knowledge about colonialism, dispossession and world endings are left to the side, while knowledge about animal movements and populations are highlighted. Indigenous understandings of the world are processed, depoliticized, sanitized and colonized into a form that is nearly unrecognizable to the Knowledge Holders who shared it in the first place. The state, and its educational institutions and research funding agencies, is interested in extracting, translating, decoding, integrating, separating, dispossessing, textualizing, documenting and sorting the knowledge of Indigenous peoples into a format that can be used to bolster the state's agenda, give the impression of collaboration and disrupt Indigenous resistance, and ultimately open up our bodies of collective understanding to Freedom of Information requests.

In short, sharing Indigenous Knowledge with the state primarily serves the state, and invests in sustaining the present colonial system of knowledge.[129] These days, I am most acutely aware of this when I talk about capitalism. My seemingly cute and quaint intimate knowledge of my territory is tolerated by agents of the state when it is used to assist scientists and civil servants to do their jobs better—when, for example, I use our oral histories as baseline data where no science exists. This tolerance might even be couched in sympathy for the world my ancestors built prior to the "arrival of the Europeans," along with some words to the effect of "wouldn't it be great if we could all live in that dream castle." But this knowledge quickly becomes recursive because these same people understand "our presently ecocidal and genocidal world as normal and unalterable."[130] They tell me that their inclusion of me and my knowledge—on their terms— makes their work more ethical and robust. What it really does is elide and remove the liberatory potential of Indigenous Knowledge systems, recasting our knowledge in service of our current "ecocidal and genocidal" world.

Indigenous Knowledge should be about our liberation—by which I mean not just the liberation of Indigenous peoples but the liberation of the planet and all the living systems that make up the earth.

It concerns me that I have come to this precise understanding; it should be inherent in all we do. It was inherent for

Gizhiigokwe. She helped to build a network for Nishnaabeg enmeshed in the existing network of life "emerging from interspecies and intercolonial schema," as Sylvia Wynter says. If, when they were focused on making our Nishnaabeg world, I had asked Gizhiigokwe what freedom means in our language, she would have responded, "Freedom from what?" If I were to ask them the same question now, I think they would have an answer, not a clarification.[131] This idea comes from Madeline Whetung. We were out walking at Jackson Creek one day and she recounted a discussion with Doug Williams in which she'd asked him for a Michi Saagiig Nishnaabeg understanding of the word *freedom*. Doug's response was, "Freedom from what?" Maddy and I laughed, and we talked about how his response made complete sense within the world that our ancestors shared. In the absence of colonialism, and in a radically egalitarian society, freedom from what, exactly?

Even in the smallest cells in my body, I always knew that I would quit the academy. Those cells knew that if I stayed within its walls, the process of writing, teaching, thinking and being within its structure would rewire my brain and harden my heart. The disciplinary nature, the institutional politics, the endless committees, the structuring of my time, my thinking and my relationships would change me and my ability to do the work I do. Had I stayed in the academy, I would not have the body of work that I do. I would not live in the world in the same way as I do. I would not think in the same way I do.

In my natural state, I live, think, analyze, read, play and sing, make and write. I never have a plan, a prospectus or a proposal. I rarely have a curriculum, and if I do, I rarely follow it. When I'm forced to write a proposal for making music, as soon as the forms are filled out, I know for certain that iteration of the album has already been ruined and died. I like the sort of teaching, or learning alongside, that occurs when the right people are in the right place at the right time.

My body of work, my life, exists in the way it does because I removed myself from the academy and the institution. I allowed my people, the land, water, anti-colonial struggle, theory and critique to structure my days in a repeated way over decades, chipping away at the "regime of truth created by capitalism" within the educational institutions that reproduce it. This has oriented my thinking and writing away from non-Indigenous allies and towards organizers, writers, scholars and thinkers engaged in struggle and working towards liberation so that we can make interconnected worlds. Worlds where we all ask, as Doug did, and as Nibi does still: Freedom from what?

19

Seeing the Forest from the Lake

One morning in 2023, I wake up to the first major snow-storm of the season. Still in bed, I scroll through the morning news to an online story detailing how the latest alleged serial killer "frequented soup kitchens and homeless shelters in Winnipeg's inner city," looking for the most vulnerable to take home and kill. He is charged with murdering four Indigenous women: Morgan Harris, Marcedes Myran, Rebecca Contois and Mashkode Bizhiki'ikwe. A group of Indigenous protesters and their allies are outside the Prairie Green landfill north of Winnipeg, demanding that it be searched for the remains of Morgan Harris and Marcedes Myran. The suspect has said that the remains are there, but Winnipeg Police say they will not do a search of the landfill.

The women were killed in May 2022.

As I read, I think: I hope no one makes this horrific story into anything other than a cause for mobilization. I don't want to listen to a true crime podcast or come across a made-for-TV movie—or anything other than blinding rage.[132]

A little later, I read an article by a Cree and Anishinaabe mother, writer and university student named Nicole Murdock. Murdock makes the excellent point that no alleged serial killer is the sole threat to Indigenous women in Winnipeg or anywhere else, and that sensationalizing the narrative of a single violent individual targeting Indigenous women fails to expose the systemic nature of such violence against Indigenous women, girls, and Two-Spirit and queer peoples.

The next morning, I find buried in the Indigenous section of my news app an article profiling Morgan Harris's daughter, Cambria. Cambria is twenty-one years old, and she has been organizing for action on MMIWG2S since she was thirteen. She tells the reporter that her mom's favourite song was Savage Garden's "Truly Madly Deeply." She says: It's a love song and she used to sing it, for the love of her kids.

I find "Truly Madly Deeply" on Spotify and play it.

At first I think I am going to cry, but by the time I get to the chorus, I am belting out the song to my kids in the "mom" way that makes teenagers recoil at the thought they are related to you.

> I wanna stand with you on a mountain
> I wanna bathe with you in the sea
> I wanna lay like this forever
> Until the sky falls down on me

Rebecca Contois "always had a heart for everything."[133]

Marcedes Myran's grandmother remembers her as "happy, smiley and trusting."[134]

And then there is Mashkode Bizhiki'ikwe.[135] Through my reading, I know Mashkode Bizhiki'ikwe Iban as Buffalo Woman—with the *Iban* in her name meaning she has passed into the spirit world. I learn from Tobi Jolly, a program coordinator at Ka Ni Kanichihk, that this woman was named by the community because her identity is unknown. This follows the practice of Grandmother Buffalo, a buffalo spirit who lends her name to those who don't yet have an Anishinaabe name.[136]

Slain is the word I encounter over and over as I comb through the debris of news articles on these four women.

Hunted is the word in my head.

I am not going to call to account here all the calculated and strategic state violences that got us to this moment, because we've already done this. Several times. Indigenous women everywhere have been organizing and mobilizing in every way imaginable for as long as I can remember, demanding action, articulating the alternatives, analyzing, studying, organizing. It was their activism that convicted Robert Pickton, who confessed to killing forty-nine people, many of them Indigenous women from the Downtown Eastside.[137] It was Indigenous women who got us an inquiry and a report that lays out what happened, and then another inquiry and a report that lays it out again. Indigenous women got us the activists and academics who took the report further than any government report could normally go.

Indigenous women know they are not safer on the streets of Winnipeg or Vancouver or Toronto or Yellowknife just because one alleged serial killer is in custody.

And yet, there is this present moment.

And in this moment: no mass mobilization. No mobilization at all outside Winnipeg.

"Truly Madly Deeply" is still playing on repeat, and it's time to drop off one of my kids at the climbing gym. As I'm scraping ice off my windshield with the edge of my health card, wearing no mitts, I'm thinking of Audra Simpson and her paper on the characterization of Theresa Spence's body throughout her fast during Idle No More and the death of Mi'kmaq woman Loretta Saunders.

Audra writes that, to settler colonial governments, the bodies of Indigenous women—and here I would add Indigenous queer people as well—"were and are sign systems and signals that could effect and affect political life." Within Audra's own Iroquois or Haudenosaunee peoples, women held, and still hold, a lot of authority and power legally and politically, forming the foundation of society. Women appointed, counselled and dehorned Chiefs, held property, and divorced men by placing their belongings outside the Longhouse.[138]

"They were the inverse of settler colonial woman."[139]

Michi Saagiig Nishnaabeg formations are very different from Haudenosaunee formations, even though we share the same ecologies, and I love that difference. Still, as I've written in *As We Have Always Done*, Nishnaabeg women and those existing outside the colonial gender binary had and have tremendous influence, and the responsibility to effect and affect political life, in our families, communities and nation. We also held, and still hold, power and authority in our society.

Audra compellingly makes the argument that in order to dispossess Indigenous peoples and maintain Indigenous dispossession, in order to secure Canada's own sovereignty, and in order to continue the stranglehold on Indigenous governance, the elimination of Indigenous women, both legally and physically, is part of settler governance and the maintenance of the state.[140]

Audra also makes the point that while there was a larger outcry online against "Pretendians" than about the murder of the four women in Winnipeg, we should avoid a hierarchy of oppression and instead see identity fraud, particularly when it is done by white women, as another form of making Indigenous lives disappear, akin to the appropriation of land, water, resources, culture and lives.[141]

As I think about Audra's words, I recall how paddling on a lake or a river immediately shifts my orientation. I see the shoreline and the land from a different perspective. In my life as it is arranged now, paddling has become an activity requiring deliberation and planning—it involves cars and canoes, calendars and scheduling. But for my ancestors, this shift in perspective from paddling on the water—a continual shift in perspective—would have been normal and ongoing. I love Audra's ability to shift, and to link seemingly individual phenomena to larger colonial systems of dispossession and disappearance. She is like her river, the St. Lawrence, flooding, swallowing drought, changing perspective and linking up to the ocean.

Being a River

Rivers are connectors. The rivers feeding into Lake Ontario and then the St. Lawrence connect me, for example, with Audra and her homeland. My people are called Michi Saagiig Nishnaabeg because we spent time at the mouths of the rivers that drain into Lake Ontario. These are rivers that travelled as raindrops and runoff through the land, into the land, down the big river to the Atlantic. They are rivers that flood in the spring to carry more and shrink in the dying summer to conserve what they carry. Expanding and contracting; a tiny creek to a magnificent ocean—making a highway where, at the end, the river doesn't exist anymore. It empties itself.

Rivers are the veins of our mother, the earth; they are the visual mapping of a watery network.

What, or where, is the centre of a network?

creek stream river lake river ocean wombs of
water, gatherings of gender non-conforming,
genderqueer, Indigiqueer, trans, Two-Spirits, queer,
lesbian, pansexual, bisexual, gay, asexual, intersex,
questioning, and everyone in between, cis-women,

cis-men, heterosexual, monogamous, polyamorous,
old people, children, neurodiverse, neurotypical,
abled and dis-abled bodies, land defenders, water
walkers, parents, pregnant people, mothers, fathers,
caretakers, language speakers, Elders, snow, knowledge holders and practitioners, hunters, trappers,
fishers, medicine people, farmers, ricers, artists,
maple trees, wild rice, salmon, pickerel, whitefish,
five-lined skinks, rain, little brown, tri-coloured
and northern long-eared bats, landings, northern map, snapping, spiny softshell, spotted and
wood turtles, American eels, monarch butterflies,
Blanchard's cricket frogs, golden eagles, bald eagles,
eastern whippoorwills, barn owls, lake sturgeon,
golden-eye lichen, boreal caribou, eastern caribou,
Algonquin wolves, American badgers, grey foxes,
wolverines, cougars, northern myotis, fawnsfoot,
eastern flowering dogwood, four-leaved milkweed,
small yellow lady's slipper, massasauga rattlesnakes,
winter, eastern white pines, tall grass prairies and
black oak savannas, Jackson Creek, Otonabee, Rice
Lake, Lake Ontario, St. Lawrence River, Atlantic
Ocean, Sargasso Sea, clouds

Nibi *decentres* itself: it leaks, moves, flows and recon-
nects, not as real estate or enclosure or property, but as a living
network, linking endless forms of life working with each
other to bring about more life, more diversity of life, more
abundance of life. Water is a matrix of bonds and attachments amongst living things of all kinds, a cascade of living
beings across time and space, on a cosmic scale, extending

into ancient times and into the future. Water is a set of practices that socially, intellectually, emotionally, spiritually and physically reproduce the planet. Practices that are deeply relational and reciprocal. Practices that embody ethics privileging kindness and gentleness, creating architectures of care across time, space and species.

The thing about a network is that the sustaining parts are not the hubs, but the connections between the hubs. Nibi, the air, the land. The thing about a network is that the individual beings aren't so important, but rather the quality and strength of the relationships between beings—so much so that the hubs, or the bodies of the network, are composed of these relationships. Life is made in the interstitial spaces between beings.

flowing
breathing
spilling
leaking
bleeding
drinking
crying

My understanding of mino-bimaadiziwin is that it decentres the idea of the human, decentres the needs, desires, knowledges and influences of humans, and favours forms of life that layer many ecologies, beyond physical bodies.

It is this understanding that leads me to ask: What if, in resisting colonialism and capitalism, we didn't focus on being recognized within the knowledge, political and ethical systems of the state, which means being recognized in the category of "human" as defined by the state? What if, instead, we obliterated the categories of gender and human and rights altogether, and created lateral, co-operative systems of sharing, all in service to bringing forth more life?

This idea of decentring, of leaking, is Anishinaabe, and many Anishinaabeg have shared it, spoken it, sung it, prayed it, written it and explained it to me, before me and alongside me. The more I think about these ideas, the more I realize that many of our stories, teachings and embodied practices, the methods we use to generate theory, are focused on continually decentring human experience—or perhaps placing human experience and our morally bankrupt knowledge systems within a plurality of other experiences and knowledges, and blurring or obliterating the boundaries between humans and all other living things. So many of our stories are about humans getting into trouble by being greedy, by thinking at the expense of feeling, by feeling at the expense of thinking, by being out of balance in some way, and plants and animals showing the way back to balance and reciprocity. In our stories, the other living beings in the network of Anishinaabeg life are teachers and co-creators. Bears never find themselves unemployed or in need of career counselling. Moose don't take over beavers' means of production. Robins don't hire other birds to get worms for them in the morning. Cardinals don't have nannies looking after their young and cleaning their nests so that their lives are more comfortable. Caribou don't have armies guarding their territory. Salmon don't stockpile food in the riverbed. The exception is always human: we are always trying to make life *more*, and this leads to the diminishment of life, it leads to less life. We humans need a lot more caretaking and intervention than other beings do, simply to function in a healthy and sustainable way within the web of life.

In our knowledge system, the Michi Saagiig Nishnaabeg share everything with all living things and their formations. We are deeply interdependent. We are intercommunal. We are but one form of life in a complex web of cascading lives. We are no more important—and many would say we are less important—than the other beings and systems making up the universe. We have no more "rights" than any other living thing in that web. We are not special, extra or exceptional. We are not owed the lives of other living things.

We are not owed the planet.

We are not owed comfortable lives.

We believe this not for self-involved reasons—not because our continuance depends upon the earth being healthy, not because our lives depend upon this, even if they do—but because, ethically, who do we think we are? Who are we to place ourselves above all other living things, most of which we don't understand? Who are we to place ourselves first when we struggle and fail so often to do what comes naturally to other forms of life?

Nishnaabemowin, the Ojibwe language, is composed mainly of verbs—words that encode the kinetics of living and our world-building practices. While there are several categories of verbs, language learners first learn two—inanimate and animate verbs—in order to be able to conjugate and speak the most basic of sentences. Animate and inanimate. Living and non-living. Beings with Spirit, and objects without life or spirit. When studying the language of a culture that is immersed in the land, finding the division between the two is not as easy as one might think. A tree is a living thing, and therefore animate. A table made of wood is an object without a spirit, and therefore inanimate. Humans, bears, and cedar are always living, even when we are dead, because our spirits have agency in the spirit world. Chairs, plastic water bottles and cars are not.

The spirit world is never an easy thing to write about, but I am compelled to do so here because it is a non-negotiable feature of Indigenous thinking and living. Within Nishnaabewin, for example, it is one of the reasons humans cannot be centred in our theorizing and living—because not only does the spirit world exist, it is always influencing everything, and is populated with the spirits of every being, plant, animal and human. Bears have knowledge. So does the five-lined skink. So do the small yellow lady's slippers. So do monarch butterflies. So do golden eagles. So do the eastern white pines. So do the Great Lakes. We make worlds in concert with all these living beings; we exist within a network of deep relationality with these living beings.

For my ancestors and my Elders, and for many water-based practitioners, Knowledge Holders and water protectors, spiritual practices provide the foundation for our interactions with other living beings. This is one reason—beyond our need for survival—that we are not all animal rights activists and vegans, for example. Our spiritual relationships allow us to negotiate the consent we need to harvest plants and animals for our continuance. It is the quality of our relationships that determines how well we are able to share, provide and caretake with other living beings around us. Some Anishinaabeg scholars such as Robin Kimmerer, Aaron Mills and Niigaanwewidam Sinclair use our practice of miinigowizin to explain how we sustain this system.

As they describe, this is a system of gift giving, of profound and endless sharing. Every living thing has a gift, and when these gifts are shared with the collective, we build a world made of gifts, whether intellectual, emotional, temporal, based on wisdom or on material being. Each life is predicated on all forms of life giving their gifts to sustain the collective. Bimaadiziwin is propelled by sharing. And reciprocity is a practice that strengthens bonds and attachments between living beings through continual sharing.

Put another way: the constant practice, both individual and communal, of redistributing "resources" or gifts within a system of Anishinaabe caretaking is a way of weaving ourselves into the network of living.

It is these relationships that continually renew the self-determination, sovereignty and freedom of the plant and animal relations with whom we humans share space in the past, present and future. And our spirits, and those of all other living things, continually reshape the boundaries of our home space, our physical bodies and our material reality, in order to form a profound and intimate connection.

This cycle takes place in the context of my favourite Nishnaabeg concept, one that Doug talked about often: Gizhewaadiziwin, the practice or the art of love, kindness, compassion to all, sharing, caring, respect, humility, tenderness. This is not romantic love, but a sense of connection, the attachment we have to one another as living beings. It is generosity, benevolence.[142]

When Indigenous peoples protest, we are motivated to put our bodies between the state and our relatives in the plant and animal world because these relatives are part of us. Our bodies are not only our bodies, but hubs of relationships in a networked web, cascading in every direction and dimension, and our spirits travel well beyond them into the cosmos of living beings.

For me, this knowledge is a tremendous asset.

It is a tremendous asset in thinking and writing about anti-colonialism and anti-capitalism. And it is a tremendous asset in living life because it invokes greater intimacy, vigorous communication and relentless honesty, a thinking-through with forms of life other than humans. From a Nishnaabewin perspective, we cannot engage in any sort of world building without that communing; it simply cannot be sustainable otherwise. Our current world is the perfect illustration of this.

Stone Canoes, Nigigoonsiwag
and Seeing Through Stone

Doug used to tell me a story about Chi'Niibish—or in English, "Big Leaf"—who lived at the narrows on Zhooni-yaagamig, or Silver Lake, about a hundred miles north of Toronto.[143] Chi'Niibish was a visionary, which meant he had the ability to see beyond current circumstances, sometimes through dreams and other times through ceremony. Dreamers and visionaries have spiritual gifts that allow them to transcend the present moment of life on earth and see beyond the horizon to other realms and other times. They generate new knowledge by communicating with spirits and ancestors, and by working with that knowledge back on earth and with the people. In our language, there are lots of different words for different kinds of dreams and visions, some of which have an embedded responsibility to share and to actualize the dream.

In his book *This Is Our Territory*, Doug wrote that Chi'Niibish's dream was for peace, and he had a set of daily practices for individuals, families and peoples to assist us in moving together through difference, disagreement and even violence towards relationships that generate more life. Peace, accountability and consent were part of a daily routine in which individuals and groups not only sorted through conflict but determined what they could give up to promote good relationships.[144] I understand this to be a project constantly in the making, in which we right relations and face conflicts as they arise, moment to moment, hour to hour, day to day.

Doug wrote that Chi'Niibish chose the Nadaweg, or the Kanien'kehá:ka (Mohawks), to work with—our neighbours with whom we share Lake Ontario, and with whom we've had times of peace as well as times of great conflict. Chi'Niibish learned Wendat or Huron, a related language to that of the Nadaweg, so he could communicate with them. He dreamed about how to build a special canoe for his journey across Lake Ontario to the heart of their homeland. The canoe he built was white, and from a distance it looked as though it was made of stone. Birchbark canoe builders know that such a craft is a difficult thing to make. Our canoes usually have the white side of the birchbark on the inside, because this is the natural way the bark curls as it dries. Inverted canoes are rarer and are used to travel to the spirit world. But Chi'Niibish built this canoe and took his Clan symbol, the eagle sitting atop a pine tree, with him on his journey.[145]

Sometimes I imagine what must have happened when Chi'Niibish told his friends that he'd dreamed of making an inverted canoe to travel across the big lake to talk peace with kin we didn't always get along with. I imagine him being met with curiosity, because the idea sounds so strange, and because my people are careful with criticism. I imagine there would have been ethical questions raised, because it might sound arrogant to decide to go, uninvited, to teach another people about peace. On the other hand, it could be seen as an act of generative accountability to face the conflict that existed between our two peoples. There would have been a few jokes made because the idea sounded preposterous. There would have been more laughter as people went about gathering spruce roots and making pitch. The kids would want to help. Someone would show the children how to split the roots, and when they got bored, they'd abandon the job and shriek around the camp. Someone would be boiling tea and cooking over the fire to feed the group that had gathered.

I imagine they would have started small, making a toy replica of the canoe to learn how to work with heat and water, to encourage the bark to bend backwards. I imagine there were prototypes that didn't quite work, and they would have had to rally past their failures and troubleshoot solutions to the problems. I imagine them scaling the replicas up gradually, until they had one that could fit Chi'Niibish and his belongings. I imagine, as they wove the canoe together, the skeptics became invested, and even if they hadn't quite believed in Chi'Niibish's vision at the start, they grew surer as they went along. They certainly believed in love and support.

I think about his departure from the shore, the gathering place where sky meets land meets water, and worlds overlap and commingle.

I wonder about those first few strokes of the paddle in this moment. Was he nervous? Did he look back?

And then I imagine the opposite view: looking out over the blue of Lake Ontario towards lake swallowing sky and seeing a stone canoe paddle closer to me. I wouldn't be able to believe what I was seeing, because of course stone doesn't float. There would be a few moments when my brain and my eyes would be in conflict, trying to figure out a plausible explanation for this defying of physics. My brain and my body would venture into a space where I'm entertaining what's possible even as I'm seeing something my brain knows to be unbelievable.

Then I think of the moment when the canoe comes into sharp visual range, and I realize it isn't made from stone but of white birchbark. Ah! That's why it floats. But also: How did he make that? Why? Why did he put such effort into working with the bark to mould it in an unnatural way? Who is this person, and why are they here, paddling towards me from the hole in the horizon?

The Michi Saagiig Nishnaabeg part of the story of Chi'Niibish ends here, or at least the part Doug told me. Chi'Niibish didn't come back to our homeland, but stayed with the Kanien'kehá:ka. The nations of the Haudenosaunee have their own magnificent archive of story and practice that came from their Peacemaker, the one who helped them achieve peace through the formation of their confederacy.[146]

Within Anishinaabewin, there are endless stories like that of Chi'Niibish—stories of people having dreams or visions or simply ideas, and then following through with a creative practice that is transformative to the larger community; stories of beings actively taking on the responsibility of the idea or dream, gathering people around who can help, and making something different together in the face of adversity. Among other insights, the story of Chi'Niibish shows the importance of nurturing our collective ability to recognize possibility or potential; it demonstrates the skill of bringing people together to support our makers in their creative sovereign practices. This is a simple process, really—

one that involves being present, noticing and being curious, believing and communing, and ultimately making—and it has built new Anishinaabe worlds and illuminated old ones. This is a generative practice of making knowledge collectively, knowledge that we need to propel us to our next iteration. And the first step in this process is both the simplest and the most difficult: being open to the possibility of seeing through the stone of the present situation.

How does our work shift when we plan and organize for the tomorrow we dream of?

Children have a knack for opening themselves to possibilities because they are not bound by ideas of reality and how the world works. It would have been effortless to convince the children around Chi'Niibish that building an inverted canoe was an excellent way to spend their time. For Anishinaabe, children are our teachers, because they are fresh from the spiritual worlds. We relish how babies teach us about gathering love together, how toddlers teach us how to say no and set boundaries, how teenagers teach us about expansion. In our tradition, when children came through the spiritual doorway to the physical earth, they were welcomed into extended families and communities. They were welcomed with an understanding of their self-determination and an ethic of non-interference—children were given the freedom to explore and learn without the confines of rigid authority, violence, or the institutions of school or church. They were woven into a society that modelled sharing knowledge and that existed without police or policing. As such, our stories tell of times when children's own self-determination made massive contributions to Anishinaabe politics, economics and knowledge.

I've written in other places about Biidaaban and the origins of maple syrup as a way of demonstrating how this process of being present, of emergence, works to generate new knowledge and nourish the entwined relationships of plants, animals and humans that make up a particular ecology or place.[147] Biidaaban brought the practice of making maple sugar to the Anishinaabe when they were out in the bush one day in March and watched a squirrel find sap. They were curious and gathered the sap in a basket. They brought their aunties to the tree for support and encouragement. They shared the sap with their Mama, who used the gift in cooking meat for the evening meal. Together, the community noticed the sugar appearing as the water evaporated, and soon this practice became a foundation of the Anishinaabe economy, a relational economy that exists within the web of life and outside racial capitalism.

I thought of this Biidaaban when I first saw a black-and-white photograph from the Archives of Ontario, taken by John Macfie in 1955, in Rebecca Belmore's *At Pelican Falls*. The photograph features a group of Anishinaabe children—I'd guess between the ages of six and eight—grouped around a boulder on the shore of a river. Their backs are to the camera. I immediately recognize their uniform buzz cuts, matching denim coveralls and workboots as markers indicating that these children are in residential school and have been sorted into a colonial gender binary and labelled as "boys" by the institution. The children are watching a white man, who is fishing with a pole. We don't know the children's relationship to this white man. We know that he is a settler by his white skin, by the way he conforms to the heteronormative dress code of the time, and perhaps because he is fishing with a pole instead of by setting a net. We don't know if he is the children's teacher or priest, or if he has no relationship to the kids.

Jessica Jacobson-Konefall, professor of Canadian Art and Theory at the School of Fine Art and Music, University of Guelph, tells us that Belmore's relationship to the photo shifted after a conversation with John Macfie, who took the photo. Macfie knew Belmore's dad; they were friends. Belmore learned that Macfie was out fishing on the river that day with his wife, and he'd taken the photo of the boys on the rock. Placing the image in the context of a friendship between Macfie and Belmore's dad adds another layer of meaning to the work.

It strikes me how interested the children are in the activity of the man who is fishing—their backs are to the camera, and we can't see their facial expressions, but their body language hints that they are still and focused. To be this transfixed is rare for kids of this age.

At first glance, I felt a sinister energy from this photo. These Indigenous children belong to generations who were stolen by the state, sent away from their families, their culture, their language and religion and knowledge system, and placed in boarding schools run by the government and churches in order to assimilate them. And there they are. Back in the arms of their parent, Aki, the earth. Back in the presence of their lifeblood, Ziibing, the river. Surrounded by the forest. Belmore says in her statement on the photo that these children reminded her of "beautiful little otters," and they remind me of this too.[148] I also see the invisible enclosure of intimate violence making them keep still and watchful, not participating. I can almost see their spirits drawn upward into the sky to meet with their ancestors and the ones who haven't yet been born. At first look, the photograph felt to me as if it captured the humiliation of the colonized—as if those little perfect otters were being mocked by the colonizer, who was fishing as a pastime on a beautiful summer day while the Anishinaabe kids, confined in a million ways, could only watch and, I hope, dream. I hoped they were dreaming of swimming and of splashing in the water. Dreaming of jumping in. Dreaming of running so fast their legs were ahead of them.

The Canadian residential school system was influenced, in part, by the Industrial Boarding School system in the United States. It was a network of boarding schools funded by the Department of Indian Affairs and administered by Christian churches[149] as part of a strategy to remove Indigenous peoples from our homelands. In this way, the state could access and extract natural resources and grow the capitalist economy and the political infrastructure it needed to replicate itself. The architecture of the residential school system was designed to convert "Indians" into heterosexual, cis-gendered, English-speaking, Christian workers who had the skills to participate in the lowest rungs of the wage economy. Residential schools operated for about a century and were purposefully located far away from the children's home communities to assist in assimilation. They were poorly funded genocidal projects, and children had to cope with malnutrition and outbreaks of infectious disease in addition to the trauma of forced removal. The schools were notoriously violent, creating generations of Indigenous peoples who are survivors of sexual, physical and emotional abuse.

In addition to the horrific individual stories of abuse, residential schools had a devastating communal impact. Parents were left mourning the loss of their children. September became the quiet time in communities as they were forced to learn to live without the laughter of any school-aged children. Extended Anishinaabe families, the communities where children participated in and learned the political and economic lifeways of our people, were devastated, and children no longer learned the ethical practices of self-determination and self-reliance, leadership and decision-making that are part of our political culture. They no longer learned the language of their parents, the one that encodes the caretaking Anishinaabe relationality. They no longer learned how to make and replicate Anishinaabe worlds—worlds that were braided into the network of living species with whom they shared time and space, worlds where individual and community self-determination were cherished, worlds where children were seen as teachers, recently arrived from the spiritual world with gifts to share and teach the community. These worlds were nearly destroyed.

Residential schools were carceral. Children couldn't leave. Families couldn't visit. Parents had no choice but to send their children away and were threatened with various consequences, including incarceration, if they resisted. In this way, residential schools, in combination with the Indian Act, contained and limited Indigenous resistance and organizing, because the state had captured the children, using them as human shields. And the intimate violence that happened within residential schools resulted in trauma that has infiltrated second and third generations of survivors' families.

The residential school at Pelican Falls was run by the Anglican Church. It was operational from 1927 to 1978 and included a 287-acre farm for the children to work. Colonialism required not only unfettered access to our land, it also needed to extract our bodies and insert them into capitalist wage labour. Boys were trained to be farmers. Girls were trained to be housewives. Two-Spirit and queer children were trained to be heterosexual and cis-gendered and form nuclear families that could reproduce the Canadian state.

The "beautiful little otters," or Nigigoonsiwag, in this photo were trapped in a series of carceral enclosures, some visible, some invisible, and some opaque. Here's what we know: they do not have control over any part of their lives, from the time they get up to the food they eat, from how they spend their day to what they learn, from what they wear to whom they are allowed to form friendships with, to what they can be in the future.

We know they can't always see the sky.

And we know they were subjected to unspeakable violence, including in some cases torture, solitary confinement, starvation and sexual abuse.[150] Many died, and their remains are buried in often unmarked graves in the vicinity of the schools.[151] At Pelican Falls residential school, the records show that 24 children, among the 150 in attendance, died between 1935 and 1946, just before the Nigigoonsiwag in the photo were there.[152] I assume some of these little people who died are older siblings and cousins of the Nigigoonsiwag:

Amos Jacob
Charles Ombash
Daniel Masakeyash

Doris Carpenter
Dorothy Ferries
Ferlin Southwind
John Wapoos
Lavina Beardy
Maggie Cromarty
Margaret Fox
Margaret Singebis
Mary Ann Ash
Mary Petawayway
Michael Jean Sapay
Mike Oombash
Morris Rooster
Nancy Tooshenan
Samuel Sakakeesic
Samuel Wesley
Stoney Johnson
Sybil Anishinabi
Thomas Ombash
Thomas Wapoos
Uriah Baxter

If all these little otters in the photo had been in an Anishinaabe community, their beautiful brown bodies would not have been trapped in the summer heat and humidity of these denim coveralls. They certainly would not have been sitting, focused, on this rock watching a white man fish. They would most certainly have been running around, laughing and yelling, playing or swimming, or in a boat or canoe, setting nets or filleting fish already caught. In these scenarios, they would have been surrounded by other children and extended family. They would be muddy from their adventures. Their gorgeous long black hair might have been braided—or might have been matted from their not being able to sit still long enough to braid it. Their gender expression and sexual orientation would have been their own decisions, and we'd see a glorious diversity of gender expressions in the photo. The community would gather and hold space around each of the Nigig as they figured out their path in life and how to contribute to their families in a way that honoured their own gifts, self-determination and interests. The river would teach them that they are connected to every other living being on the planet, and that you can transform into different states of being, and that you can travel far and still belong if you know how to weave connections. The sky would bathe them in possibilities. The air would teach them that the container they are held in is both leaky and connected, and is strengthened through deep relationality.

A few of them would have been driven to be creative, and this would have been noticed by their relatives. The family's responsibility would have been to hold space around those little makers, providing encouragement and support as they learned to live within the power of their body and voice and connected these to the world around them, making work that reflected, elevated and challenged the community. This, too, is a practice of love, of connecting and belonging. A few of them would have been dreamers and visionaries like Chi'Niibish, and their relatives would have been responsible for seeing this gift, helping them hone their skills, and, most importantly, believing in them.

So here the Nigigoonsiwag are, on the side of the river. Maybe their ancestors are awakening them in their bones. They are feeling the heat of Niibin. They are seeing Ziibing. They are surrounded by trees, and perhaps they can hear the falls. They are watching a man fish, which is a clue to another way of living. Maybe the moment we are witnessing in this photo is when Nigigoonsiwag see through the stone of their diminished daily life in residential school.

Maybe they are dreaming beyond their present moment.

Oral stories and archival documents teach us that Indigenous children most certainly dreamed of worlds other than the ones they were forced to live in at residential schools. We know the story of Chanie Wenjack, another Nigigoons, who escaped from Cecilia Jeffrey Indian Residential School in Kenora, Ontario, not too far from Pelican Falls.[153] In the early 1960s, Chanie tried to walk the six hundred kilometres from Kenora to his home in Ogoki Post on the Marten Falls reserve. The twelve-year-old and two friends, Ralph and Jackie MacDonald, travelled thirty-one kilometres the first day and made it to the home of Charles Kelly, the MacDonald boys' uncle. After some days of rest, and carrying food, matches and advice from the Kellys, Chanie Wenjack continued his journey, following the Canadian National rail lines. He had found a passenger timetable that included a map, and he used it as a guide.

Chanie walked for thirty-six more hours, covering another twenty kilometres. But October in northern Ontario can get cold and Chanie didn't have proper clothing for the journey. He died before he made it into the arms of his parents. Many, many children—some estimates say as many as thirty thousand—didn't make it home. They died in these schools from abuse, malnutrition, disease; and they died from trying to walk themselves to a better life.[154]

Chanie, like many Indigenous, Black and Palestinian children, died seeing through the stone.

In our present moment, during a time that includes the spectacular violence of the Israeli apartheid state, I tell myself that I must also see through the stone of colonial states and corporate media. If I shut out the noise of those intent on genocide and close my eyes and listen, I see those Gazan children, those beautiful little Palestinian olive seedlings, and their laughter; I see the press conference[155] in which some spoke of their hopes and dreams for a future full of school and the beach. I see their tiny hands waving white flags as they are led away from their worlds. I see them walking through Israeli checkpoints with their siblings on their way to school in places like Al Khalil (Hebron). I see them mourning the loss of their parents, friends, cousins and families. I see them mourning the loss of limbs. And I see them becoming journalists on TikTok and Instagram. I see their anger, their pain and their resistance.

I see that their open-air prison is also full of love and belonging and schools and libraries and football games and beaches and toys and fun. I see them painting and drawing on the rubble-reduced walls of their former homes, making worlds out of nothing. I see a "place of a million plots and a thousand narratives; where fear is the norm and joy is loud, raucous, and unapologetic; where amputees are more commonplace than washing machines and spent tear-gas grenades are used as strawberry pots."[156]

These children in Gaza are practising "Seeing through the Stone" of Israeli apartheid.

And I am practising seeing them, through the stone of colonial lies.

When the children of Gaza look up, do they see a sky that is aiming to eliminate them, or perhaps choke their lungs with smoke and debris from carpet bombing? Do they see leaflets and white phosphorus?

> *I grant you and the little ones refuge,*
> *the little ones who*
> *change the rocket's course*
> *before it lands*
> *with their smiles.*[157]

The cage of spectacular violence Gazan children are living in, and dreaming beyond, is different from the cage of Anishinaabe children in the photo at Pelican Falls, and from the Black and Brown children in cages at the borders between nation-states.

Different and entwined.

Different and related.

> *Invaders   came back once again,*
> *claimed the land*
> *with   fists and fire excuses beliefs*
> *of the chosen and the promised*
> *as if God is a real-estate agent.*[158]

These children are related through love of land, family and culture. They are related through rivers and seas, springs and trees, as long as the grass grows and the sun shines.

And they are related through invaders, who act as if "God is a real-estate agent."

In Alexis Pauline Gumbs's book *Undrowned*, Alexis tells us that dolphin mothers sing to their babies while they are in the womb as well as after they are born so that the babies can learn their names. Learning their names is a way of recognizing their belonging and connection to their kin, the ones who will protect and take care of them.[159] She tells us that the rest of the pod gathers quietly round as the mother sings to support this process. I think of the baby dolphin listening through their womb-home to a world they cannot yet see and perhaps cannot even imagine, hearing through stone. Learning to cut through the noise of boat traffic and capitalism to hear the frequency of belonging.

With this dolphin love story lodged in our hearts, Alexis continues, in true Black feminist form, to contrast this dolphin birth practice with the birth of human beings who are being held in captivity. This is a carceral practice that takes place daily in the United States and Canada, where the state shackles incarcerated people who are giving birth and apprehends their children almost immediately. Alexis goes on to link this reality to that of young asylum seekers who are separated from their parents in cages at the border between the United States and Mexico, and to the more than five million American children with parents in prison.

Now I extend Gumbs's thinking: this connects us to the hundreds of thousands of Indigenous and Black children apprehended by the state and placed in care.[160] And this connects us to Palestinian children martyred in Gaza, walking through checkpoints in Al Khalil, held in jails without charges in the West Bank, or displaced with their families in the diaspora.

A little while ago, I travelled to Australia to visit with Indigenous peoples there, who have a related experience of colonialism and slavery. I arrived in Meanjin (Brisbane), in Yugara Country, to attend a day of the Sisters Inside Conference. I didn't have much time in Meanjin, so the first thing I did after dropping my belongings at the hotel was walk to the Queensland Art Gallery to see a show called *sis: Pacific Art 1980–2023*, a show that celebrates the work of women artists from across the Pacific. I was there specifically to see a sculpture by Taloi Havini.

Taloi Havini is from the Nakas tribe of the Hakö people, and was born in Arawa, in the Autonomous Region of Bougainville. As a child, she was exiled with her family to Australia because of her parents' political organizing; they had been part of an independence movement resisting the destruction of their homeland from copper mining by multinational Rio Tinto and the government of Papua New Guinea. Taloi's piece in the show was called *Beroana (shell money)*, *2015*, and it was a stunning visual sculpture of the Hakö economy.

When I entered the space, I saw a huge, fragile spiral suspended from the ceiling of the gallery, starting at a single point near the floor and flowing upwards to the sky. The spiral is made from a series of shells strung together like beads. These are shells that Taloi's people used, and still use, to trade with each other in a horizontal economy that privileges care and interdependence over wealth—or perhaps *as* wealth. Havini made each replica shell by hand from stoneware, then strung the shells together as a visual representation of an exchange economy governed by individual and collective self-determination and deep reciprocity.

Experiencing *Beroana*, I felt grounded. I had a sense that I was part of something bigger than myself, experiencing economy as belonging, as a spiral pulling me out of myself and weaving me into the cosmos. I was reminded that Indigenous economic practices are not a hoarding of material and resources for the few; they are a connected spiralling out to form a leaky, permeable container that is expansive and responsive and designed to meet the needs of all living things. I got a sense, standing there, that my existence is an intimate network within my immediate environment, and is connected, even across vast oceans and distance, to others. Together we spiral upwards towards the sky, through our differences, becoming the planet and the cosmos.

And it struck me: in this sculpture, in this economy, in the Hakö world these practices built, there is *no* stone to see through.

In the world Havini and her people build, putting children into cages at borders or in schools is unthinkable. Bombing children and their families relentlessly is unspeakable. Incarcerating children without charges and indefinitely is horrific. Birth is not a medical event but a ceremony, as life passes through one realm to another. Parents singing to babies is sacred. The laughter and joy of children playing on the beach at Beit Lahia or in Cape Town or on Manhattan Beach or in Pelican Lake is the result of cultures and politics that cherish their joy and freedom.

Colonialism, in contrast, is about severing relationships—to each other, to our lands, to hope and to our futures. In its faceless face, I'm gathering the dolphins, the beautiful little olive saplings, the Nigigoonsiwag, the children apprehended at all the borders, and these *Beroana*, into Chi'Niibish's stone canoe. Together, we'll dream and build worlds where we'll call the aesthetics of abolition normal, and we'll no longer have to envision liberation because we'll be living it, and it will be all we know.

The One That Cleans the World

I carry a river. It is who I am: 'Aha Makav.[161]

Nibi. The one that cleans the world. The one that does the unglamorous, underappreciated, unseen labour of washing and tidying up, the work that no one else will do.

Nibi. The blood of the planet, merging through subterranean and atmospheric vessels and circuitry.

Nayaano-nibiimaang Gichigamiin is heart, lungs, kidneys and liver, pumping, mixing, detoxing, carrying the past to the future.

Nibi is medicine, a daily streaming for our circumnavigation.

When our Elders say, "Water is sacred," they mean it is work on a scale beyond our comprehension.

They mean, Nibi is not disposable.

Nibi is not capital.

Nibi is a provocateur, enacting a theory and a body of knowledge about how to live inside the cacophony of living.

She carries the river. I carry the ice. You carry an ocean. She carries a glacier. They carry the snow. He carries a marsh.

Hir carries the breath. It carries the spring. We (excluding them) carry the waterfall. We (including them) carry the waves.

And while in this moment Nibi might be hurt—horribly contaminated and reeling from the ongoing assaults of capitalism—left alone, we believe, as do many other Indigenous peoples, Nibi will eventually revive itself. Filtering, regenerating and renewing is already threaded through the web. Nibi may take a very long time and require an absolute rewiring of humanity, but we believe Nibi regenerates.

Nibi, and its unquenchable thirst for mino-bimaadiwizin, lives in resistance to disposability despite being bought and sold, drained and contained, diverted and dammed. Nibi is a fugitive, raining down a quest for renewal, cycling through time and across every border.

Nibi is speaking through action, critiquing by making an alternative. Nibi's theory, the theory of water, is a scathing indictment of every part of the death machine that has led to this present moment.

Nibi rains down on capitalist scaffoldings, revealing captured beings who are separated from the network of life, their value in terms of capital extracted, their bodies withering into disposability. Spruce, pine, hemlock and Douglas fir, their woody bodies destroyed into lumber or pulp. Prairies tortured into farmland. Rivers incarcerated into hydroelectric dams. Land confiscated into highways, roads, pipelines, railways, housing, golf courses and parks. Gold-silver, nickel-copper, copper-zinc, lead-zinc, iron, molybdenum, uranium, potash and diamond captured and mined. Shale arrested into oil, gas and bitumen. Salmon, herring and halibut dispossessed from oceans.

What is left is fire, smoke, flood and catastrophe. Collapsing ecological systems with cascading, magnifying, collateral death.

> *When a Mohave says,* Inyech 'Aha Makavch ithuum, *we are saying our name. We are telling a story of our existence.* The river runs through the middle of my body.[162]

Nishnaabeg grandparents held on to things. Twist-ties, tiny pieces of fishing line, scraps of material, buttons, cardboard, plastic food containers, newspapers, old cars and snowmobiles, one-litre milk bags (all bags, actually), elastic bands, jars, cans, and I could go on and on. Anything that was designed for one use was (and still is) washed, taped or dried and used again and again. Something not useful in the moment may be useful in the future to repair, fix, recycle or reuse in some way. Part of this habit was motivated by poverty, but part of it is motivated by love.

The river runs through my body and tells the story of my existence. "The one that cleans the world" runs through me,[163] and reveals the story of my existence.

These saved elastic bands.

What happens when we write the analysis of what capitalism is, and how it works, from the perspective of those who caretake the world? From the point of view of hunters and trappers and those who tan moose hides? From the position of those Missing and Murdered Indigenous Women and Girls, and 2SQ people, or those people who are the targets of the most severe forms of colonial violence? What do we learn when we re-centre the analysis of capitalism from the knowledge of those Indigenous women and 2SQ people whose lands, bodies, lives, languages, knowledge systems and spiritualities were stolen; whose children, parents, grandchildren and grandparents were stolen; who live with housing and food insecurity, limited access to health care and diminished joy; whose lives were stolen, eliminated, made invisible or shrunk so that the lives of white bourgeois women around the world are comfortable?[164]

We learn what our ancestors lived: that capitalism is incommensurable with Indigenous life.

When Mojaves say the word for tears, *we return to our word for* river, *as if our river were flowing from our eyes.*[165]

Our river is flowing from my eyes. Our river in my body, shattered into dams and lift locks, pipes and pumping, pools and sprinklers, is flowing from my eyes.

We must go until we smell the black root-wet anchoring the river's mud banks. We must go beyond beyond to a place where we have never been the center, where there is no center—beyond, toward what does not need us yet makes us.[166]

to unseparate
to beyond
towards
to braid with land and sky
to blue
to shimmer
to mouth into again

toward what does not need us yet makes us. [167]

A Theory of Water

It is coming up on two years since Doug passed away, and in writing this book I've fallen into the creation story he left. Retelling it. Thinking about it. Carrying it. Playing it in the background of life, over and over. Recalling the details on different continents. Hearing his voice in mine. Letting the story wander and leak further outside his container and deeper into mine. I've pulled out the pieces and spread them out on the hardwood floor and watched the sunlight travel across the room and through the pieces. His story has permeated this one—not exactly the same, but related.

I've taken this origin story off the island. I've taken it to Falastin and Ohcejohka, Meanjin, Narrm, Warrane, Tarntanya, Denendeh and Amsterdam. I've been sintering it. Finding myself inside it. Finding the present in it by shifting the story from text to sound and back to text. Listening to the present from inside Gzhwe Manidoo or Gizhiigokwe. Nibi or Mikinak.

In Meanjin, or Brisbane, I met the writer and thinker Andrea Ritchie for a drink. This was November 2023, a beginning of terrible times, as the Israel Nakba machine, flanked by the United States and Canada, tested the world with what they could get away with, the violence and unspeakable atrocities. We talked about how bad things were, and how they would get worse. We talked about what needs to be done. I told her how I saw the emergent strategies she wrote about in *Practicing New Worlds* inside Nishnaabeg thought too—even inside my own writing, and that of others, in *Dancing on Our Turtle's Back, As We Have Always Done* and *Rehearsals for Living*. I described how the Elders I had worked with in northern Ontario, in Manitoba and in my own territory were always more concerned with getting the right people to the right place at the right time, and seeing what emerged, than with hanging on tightly to logistics or curriculum. I said that in the land-based education I participate in, I was always advocating for curriculum and learning objectives to be left behind, and for educators to bring ingredients—Elders, learning, land and water—together, and then see what learning emerges from that alchemy.

After I got back to my hotel from my visit with Andrea, I thought about Gzhwe Manidoo setting out to make the world right now, in our wreckage, using their dream as the blueprint. I thought about all their failures, and how the world they instantly created looked great initially, as such worlds always do, being linear projects. But then they got into trouble and were surrounded by a contaminated swamp of failure and death.

Gzhwe Manidoo grieved but did not give up. They adapted and stayed the course. They, Gzhwe Manidoo, are iterative. Rejecting isolation, they found themselves inside difference, inside Gizhiigokwe.

Gizhiigokwe, too, is iterative. By sintering, Gzhwe Mani-doo and Gizhiigokwe learned that in isolation they didn't have the whole picture. They needed to work together to make possibilities for more life, and then with all the forms of life they were creating to continually renew the world.

Nibi as adaptation. Watching as listening. Listening as feeling. Feeling as acting. Morphing from ice to rain to water vapour. Shifting from glacier to ocean to ripples and pools to the glistening of dew. Nibi has never given up. Their resilience is unmatched. If they are captured, they transform. If they are contaminated, they clean.

Nibi acted.

Gizhiigokwe acted.

Chi'Mikinak acted.

They were surrounded by a fractal, which reminded them that life looks the same across scales. Small-scale embodiment of the vision moves the larger collective towards the whole vision.[168]

They needed a map—but in that ocean of water, they were surrounded by maps.

Loon acted.

Otter acted.

Muskrat acted.

Because loon, otter, muskrat and Gizhiigokwe had sintered, they knew each other and became a symphony.

They put dirt on the back of the turtle and grew the earth. They had self-determination over their own bodies and in their own communities. Gizhiigokwe made iteration her spine and became the moon, reminding us that every night, every single night of this story, we must live in a way that creates more possibilities for life.

Gzhwe Manidoo, Gizhiigokwe and Nibi hide clues and reminders of this everywhere. And Nibi lives them all, embodying practice.

Some revolts are incremental, eroding, melting, freezing, seeping, leaking.

Politics that are fractal, adaptive, non-linear and iterative, resilient and transformative, interdependent and decentralized, all move towards more possibilities for life.

Human worlds that are fractal, adaptive, non-linear and iterative, resilient and transformative, interdependent and decentralized, all move towards more possibilities for life.

Solidarities that are fractal, adaptive, non-linear and iterative, resilient and transformative, interdependent and decentralized, all move towards more possibilities for life.

An Indigenous internationalism, which is at once hyperlocal and global, encompasses all life on the planet.

It is a presence and a presencing.

It connects all living things. It cycles and reproduces the planet. Nibi's theories are all around us, all the time, the most magnificent manifestation of mino-bimaadiziwin.

It is a Theory of Water, and it lives inside all of us.

ACKNOWLEDGEMENTS

Chi'miigwech to Madeline Whetung and to Vida, for laughing, walking, thinking and being Michi Saagiig Nishnaabeg with me, and to Maddy for providing comments on an early draft.

Miigwech to Bonnie Devine, for quiet moments with Rebecca Belmore's *Wave Sound* at the McMichael Gallery in the fall of 2022. Chi'miigwech to Rebecca Belmore for an astounding body of work.

Thank you to the Canada Council for the Arts for their support.

Sections of the chapter "Listening in Our Present Moment" were published in "Rebecca Belmore" in *Early Days: Indigenous Art from the McMichael*, edited by Bonnie Devine, John Geoghegan and Sarah Milroy (Vaughan, ON: Figure 1 Publishing, 2023), pp. 283–88.

A previous version of "Pinery Road and Concession 11" was published in volume 46 of the journal *Topia* (March 2023): 232–37.

An earlier version of "Stone Canoes, Nigigoonsiwag and Seeing Through Stone" was published in the exhibition catalogue for *Seeing through Stone*, San José Museum of Art, San José, California. Thanks to Gina Dent and Rachel Nelson for including my work.

My deepest gratitude to Lynn Henry and Dionne Brand for their careful, thoughtful and generous editing of this book, and to Jackie Kaiser for helping me bring this book to these two beautiful minds. Chi'miigwech to Christi Belcourt for the use of her artwork on the cover.

NOTES

CHAPTER 1: *When It Was Icy, I Could Fly*

1   See the Ojibwe People's Dictionary, ojibwe.lib.umn.ed /main-entry/zhooshkodaabaan-na.

2   Inuvik Ski Club, "Club History," www.inuvikskiclub.ca /home/club-history.

3   Pavlina Sudrich, "Skiing, God and Father Mouchet," *Yukon News*, December 6, 2013.

4   Several survivors' stories were on a blog called "Sylvia's Site."

5   Jess Dunkin, "The Finest Spring Skiing in the World," *Up Here*, March 2018, uphere.ca/articles/finest-spring -skiing-world.

6   Ibid.

7   Sudrich, "Skiing, God and Father Mouchet."

CHAPTER 2: *Nibi*

8   See page 85 in Andrea J. Ritchie's *Practicing New Worlds: Abolition and Emergent Strategies* (Chico, CA: AK Press,

2023), and my own thoughts on emergence in *Dancing on Our Turtle's Back* (Winnipeg: ARP Books, 2011).

CHAPTER 3: *Listening in Our Present Moment*

9   Dionne Brand, *Nomenclature: New and Collected Poems* (Toronto: McClelland & Stewart, 2022), p. 26.

10 Wanda Nanibush, "An Interview with Rebecca Belmore," *Decolonization: Indigeneity, Education & Society* 3, no. 1 (2014): 214.

11 See Marjorie Beaucage's short film Ayum-ee-aawach Oomamamowan, filmed at the Wiggins Bay Blockade, August 1992.

12 This idea is Dionne Brand's and comes from her conversation with David Naimon in the podcast *Between the Covers*, tinhouse.com/transcript/between-the-covers-dionnebrand-interview/, accessed July 27, 2024.

13 Clark MFA in Visual Arts, "Art Talk: Rebecca Belmore," *YouTube*, January 11, 2021, www.youtube.com/watch?v=9yjogRaH_oE&t=1131s.

14 Lindsay Nixon, "Rebecca Belmore Wants Us to Listen to the Land," *Canadian Art*, June 7, 2017.

15 See Michael Belmore discussing his use of copper here: "Michael Belmore: Smoulder," Mackenzie Art Gallery website, mackenzie.art/learn/studio-sundays/michael-belmore-smoulder/, accessed July 27, 2024. And Iris Blake's dissertation discussing *Wave Sound* and the aesthetic echoes in response to audience: Iris Sandjette Blake, "Unsettling the Coloniality of Voice" (PhD diss., University of California Riverside, 2020), 119–20,

escholarship.org/content/qt49h1c8r2/qt49h1c8r2_no
-Splash_cbb4006767345d120dbf9474ca9b10e5.pdf.

16   You can listen to sound recordings here: Art Gallery
      of Ontario, "Rebecca Belmore: Wave Sound Audio,"
      Soundcloud, July 10, 2018, soundcloud.com/agotoronto
      /sets/rebecca-belmore-wave-sound-audio.

17   Blake, "Unsettling the Coloniality," 109.

18   A different and truncated version of this piece was com-
      missioned for the catalogue *Early Days: Indigenous Art at
      the McMichael*, ed. Bonnie Devine, John Geoghegan and
      Sarah Milroy (Kleinburg, ON: Figure 1 Publishing and the
      McMichael Canadian Art Collection, 2023). Bonnie Devine
      took me to see the piece in the McMichael in fall 2022.

CHAPTER 4: *Sintering*

19   Will Pearson, "Climate Change Will Bring More Flood
      Waters Downtown. How Much Will the $52 Million
      Jackson Creek Diversion Help?," *Peterborough Currents*,
      December 13, 2021.

20   Doug Williams (as told to Julie Kapyrka), "The Chemong
      Portage," *Kawartha Promoter*, March 20, 2019.

21   American Avalanche Association/National Avalanche
      Center, "Settlement," Avalanche.org, avalanche.org
      /avalanche-encyclopedia/settlement/, accessed July 28, 2024.

22   Trinity Social Justice Initiative, "Conjuncture: Against
      Pessimism," *YouTube*, August 22, 2022, socialjusticeinitiative
      domains.trincoll.edu/uncategorized/episode-1-season-2/.

23   Niloufar Nematollahi, "The Revolt in Iran Is Rallying Its
      Diverse Working Class," *Jacobin*, March 26, 2023.

CHAPTER 5: *Gizhiigokwe & Chi'Mikinak*

24 Doug Williams, *Michi Saagiig Nishnaabeg: This Is Our Territory* (Winnipeg: ARP Books, 2018), pp. 24–27.

25 This section is entirely based on Williams, *Michi Saagiig Nishnaabeg*, pp.13–15.

26 This section is entirely based on Williams, *Michi Saagiig*.

27 Noelani Goodyear-Kaōpua, "Ku'oko'a Independence," *The Value of Hawai'i 3*, ed. Noelani Goodyear-Kaōpua, Craig Howes, Jonathan Kay Kamakawiwoole Osorio and Aiko Yamashiro (Honolulu: University of Hawaii Press, 2020), pp.17–21.

28 See also Dian Million, "Felt Theory: An Indigenous Feminist Approach to Affect and History," *Wicazo Sa Review* 24, no. 2 (2009): 53–76.

29 Goodyear-Kaōpua, "Ku'oko'a Independence."

30 This section is entirely based on my own interpretation of Williams, *Michi Saagiig Nishnaabeg*, pp. 13–15.

CHAPTER 6: *Mappings of the Liminal*

31 Joshua Myers, *Cedric Robinson: The Time of the Black Radical Tradition* (Medford, MA: Polity Press, 2021), pp. 1–13.

32 Kimbwandende K.B. Fu-Kiau, *African Cosmology of the Bantu-Kongo: Principles of Life and Living*, 2nd ed. (n.p.: African Tree Press and Athelia Henrietta Press, 2001).

33 Williams, *Michi Saagiig Nishnaabeg*, p. 32.

34 "Earth's Fresh Water," *National Geographic*, accessed January 26, 2024, education.nationalgeographic.org/resource/earths-fresh-water.

35 "How Long Does the Water Cycle Really Take?," *Science*

World, October 8, 2014, www.scienceworld.ca/stories
/how-long-does-water-cycle-really-take/.

CHAPTER 7: *Un-mappings Leading to Everywhere and Nowhere*

36 Saidiya Hartman, *Wayward Lives, Beautiful Experiences:
Intimate Histories of Social Upheaval* (Toronto: Penguin
Random House, 2019). For more information on the gath-
ering, see maptothedoorat20.com/about/.

37 *Undrowned* is a reference to Alexis Pauline Gumbs's book of
the same name.

38 See Andrea A. Davis, *Horizon, Sea, Sound: Caribbean &
African Women's Cultural Critiques of Nation* (Evanston, IL:
Northwestern University Press, 2022).

39 "Change the air" is a phrase from Dionne Brand, "Dionne
Brand: On Narrative, Reckoning and the Calculus of
Living and Dying," *Toronto Star*, July 4, 2020.

CHAPTER 8: *Pinery Road and Concession 11*

40 A previous version of this chapter was published in *Topia*
as part of the special issue on *Map at 20*.

41 See "Making Baskets with Nokomis" in Williams, *Michi
Saagiig Nishnaabeg*, pp. 22–23.

42 This line came out of a discussion between me, Christina
Sharpe and Dionne Brand on April 28, 2022. They began
to teach me how to pay homage to, how to memorialize,
celebrate and mark the lives of our missing and murdered,
and here I am trying. I am grateful to both of them, and
the idea of "the one that" comes from Christina Sharpe's
forthcoming book. See Annette Francis, "Family of Cileana

Taylor Wants Charges against Boyfriend Upgraded," *APTN National News*, March 26, 2021.

43 Williams, *Michi Saagiig Nishnaabeg*, pp.18–19.

44 See Brand, "Dionne Brand: On Narrative."

45 Williams, *Michi Saagiig Nishnaabeg*, p. 76.

46 "You notice its width" in Dionne Brand, *A Map to the Door of No Return: Notes to Belonging* (Toronto: Penguin Random House, 2011), p. 145.

47 I learned this idea from Fred Moten and Stephano Harney, "Give Your House Away, Constantly," *Millennials Are Killing Capitalism* (podcast), July 11, 2020.

48 See the Ojibwe People's Dictionary, ojibwe.lib.umn.edu /main-entry/akii-mazina-igan-ni.

49 Brand, *A Map to the Door of No Return*, p. 143.

50 Ibid., p. 145.

CHAPTER 9: *"Where My Mother Held Me"*

51 Tariq Luthun, *How the Water Holds Me* (Durham, NC: Bully City Press, 2020), p. 10.

52 Madeline Whetung, "At the Shore: Everyday Anti-violences and the Practice of Queer Creation in Michi Saagiig Nishnaabeg Territory," PhD diss., (University of British Columbia, 2023).

53 Katsi has been writing and speaking about this since I was a PhD student in the late 1990s. Here is a more recent example: www.talkingleaves.org/node/61.

54 M. NourbeSe Philip, "The Ga(s)p," in *Poetics and Precarity*, ed. Myung Mi Kim and Cristanne Miller (Albany: State University of New York, 2018), p. 31.

55 Madeline Whetung, "(En)gendering Shoreline Law:

Nishnaabeg Relational Politics along the Trent Severn
Waterway," *Global Environmental Politics* 19, no. 3 (2019):
16–32, https://doi.org/10.1162/glep_a_00513.

56   Ibid.

57   Shannon Webb-Campbell, "Reclaiming Indigenous
Territories, Bead by Bead," *Canadian Art*, June 27, 2017.

58   Lisa Myers, "Water Is Land, Land Is Also Water," *C Magazine*,
June 1, 2017.

59   Webb-Campbell, "Reclaiming Indigenous Territories."

60   Whetung, "(En)gendering Shoreline Law."

61   Ibid.

CHAPTER 10: *Agaming: On the Shore*

62   Whetung, "At the Shore."

63   Whetung, "(En)gendering Shoreline Law."

64   Robin Wall Kimmerer, *Braiding Sweetgrass: Indigenous
Wisdom, Scientific Knowledge and the Teachings of Plants*
(Minneapolis: Milkweed Editions, 2013), pp. 225–32.

65   A. Husain, J. Reddy, D. Bisht, et al., "Fractal Dimension of
Coastline of Australia," *Scientific Reports* 11, no. 6304 (2021),
https://doi.org/10.1038/s41598-021-85405-0.

66   See *The Shoreline Dilemma*, Toronto Biennial of Art
program, September 21–December 1, 2019; and *Water,
Kinship, Belief*, ed. Tairone Bastien, Candice Hopkins and
Katie Lawson, co-published by the Toronto Biennial of
Art and Art Metropole Publication, April 2022, essays by
Candice Hopkins, pp. 61–91; Tairone Bastien, 91–113;
Katie Lawson, 113–45; Camille Turner and Yaniya Lee,
33–41; and Lexicon, 41–69; and all the works within the
biennial and this catalogue.

CHAPTER 11: *Bull Frogs, Cattails and Water Lilies*

67   Williams, *Michi Saagiig Nishnaabeg*, pp. 87–91.

68   Ibid., p. 87.

69   "Wetlands," Ontario Nature website, ontarionature.org
      /campaigns/wetlands/, accessed July 31, 2024.

70   "Global Wetland Outlook," Ramsar Convention on
      Wetlands website, www.global-wetland-outlook.ramsar.
      org/, accessed July 31, 2024; "Wetlands," Ontario Nature.

71   "Wetlands," Ontario Nature.

CHAPTER 12: *"Remembering Where It Used to Be"*

72   "'Floods' is the word they use, but in fact it is not flooding:
      it is remembering. Remembering where it used to be.
      All water has a perfect memory and is forever trying to
      get back to where it was," is a quote from Toni Morrison
      from a talk she gave at the New York Public Library in
      1986. "The Charlotte-Mecklenburg Story," Charlotte
      Mecklenburg Library website, www.cmstory.org/exhibits
      /african-american-album-volume-2/1996-toni-morrison
      -speaks-library, accessed July 31, 2024.

73   David Lees, "Eels on Wheels," *Walrus*, December 2008.

74   R. MacGregor, J. Casselman, L. Greig, J. Dettmers, W.A.
      Allen, L. McDermott and T. Haxton, *Recovery Strategy
      for the American Eel (*Anguilla rostrata*) in Ontario*, Ontario
      Recovery Strategy Series prepared for Ontario Ministry
      of Natural Resources (Peterborough, 2013); and Elder
      (Dr.) William Commanda, *Manoshkadosh, The American
      Eel: A Circle of All Nations Note* (Perth, ON: Community
      Stewardship Council of Lanark County, 2010).

75   www.fws.gov/northeast/newsroom/Americaneel9.26
      .11.2.pdf.

76   MacGregor et al., *Recovery Strategy*; Helen Briggs, "Eel
      Migration Study Tells 'Romantic' Tale," *BBC News*,
      October 5, 2016.

77   Commanda, *Manoshkadosh*.

78   Ibid.

79   Ibid.

80   *Swim Drink Fish* (blog), www.waterkeeper.ca/case
      -american-eel, accessed July 31, 2024.

81   Lees, "Eels on Wheels."

82   Ibid.

83   Alexis Pauline Gumbs, *Undrowned: Black Feminist Lessons
      from Marine Mammals* (Chico, CA: AK Press, 2021), pp. 6–7.

84   Raj Bhattacharya, "Sargasso Sea," *Bermuda Attractions*,
      www.bermuda-attractions.com/bermuda2_000142.htm,
      accessed July 31, 2024.

85   Ibid.

CHAPTER 13: *Maps to Statelessness*

86   Steve Salaita, "So You're a Professor? Here's What You
      Can Do to Oppose Genocide," *Steve Salaita* (blog), January 7,
      2024, stevesalaita.com/so-youre-a-professor-heres-what
      -you-can-do-to-oppose-genocide/.

87   Christi Belcourt, "Mapping Roots," *Christi Belcourt*
      (artist's website), www.christibelcourt.com/Gallery
      /gallerySERIESmrPage1.html, accessed August 1, 2024.

88   Mimi Gellman, "The Poetics of Indigenous Carto-
      Activism," *C Magazine*, Issue 150, p. 39.

89   Ibid., pp. 41–42.

90 Maureen Gruben in conversation with Kyra Kordoski, *C Magazine*, Issue 150, p.52.

91 Chippewas of Rama First Nation, "Alan Ojiig Corbiere: The Underlying Importance of Wampum Belts . . . ," *YouTube*, March 30, 2015, www.youtube.com/watch?v =wb-RftTCQ_8.

92 According to Corbiere, another interpretation refers to strings, and yet another is that of a harness or a device used to carry things out of the bush. See Chippewas of Rama First Nation, "Alan Ojiig Corbiere."

93 Audra Simpson, *Mohawk Interruptus: Political Life across the Borders of Settler States* (Durham, NC: Duke University Press, 2014), p. 148.

94 Winona LaDuke, *The Winona LaDuke Reader* (Penticton, BC: Theytus Books, 2002), pp. 79–80.

CHAPTER 14: *"All of Them Carrying Yesterday"*

95 A previous version of this chapter was published in 2021 in Austria in English and German, in *Camera Austria* 156, camera-austria.at/zeitschrift/156-2021/.

96 "Sacred Ojibwa Scrolls Found after 70 Years," *CBC News*, May 9, 2000.

97 "The Headwaters of the Mississippi River in Ojibwe," The Decolonial Atlas, January 12, 2015, decolonialatlas .wordpress.com/2015/01/12/the-headwaters-of-the -mississippi-river-in-ojibwe/.

98 Lucille Clifton, "The Mississippi River Empties into the Gulf," in *How to Carry Water* (New York: BOA Editions, 2020), p. 167.

99   Like Clifton's poem, Saidiya Hartman's forward, to
     William C. Anderson's *The Nation on No Map*, calls me
     to think alongside her when she writes that "Anarchism"
     unfolds *with and as* Black feminism and Indigenous struggle.
     The full context is here: "'Anarchism' is an open word
     whose contours and meaning are shaped by the long
     struggle for Black Liberation, by the centuries-long resistance
     to racial slavery, settler colonialism, capitalism, state violence,
     genocide and anti-Blackness. 'Anarchism' gathers and
     names the practices of mutual aid and the program for
     survival that have sustained us in the face of unimaginable
     violence. It unfolds with and as Black feminism and
     Indigenous struggle. It offers a blueprint for radical trans-
     formation, for the possibilities of existence beyond the
     world of scarcity and managed depletion, enclosure and
     premature death."

100 William C. Anderson, *The Nation on No Map: Black
     Anarchism and Abolition* (Chico, CA: AK Press, 2021), p. xiii.

101 Ibid., p.15.

102 Ibid., p. xiv.

103 Ibid., p. xxiii.

104 Ibid.

105 The next thing Anderson does is also part of the beautiful
     practice of dabaadendiziwin, and that is he tells the readers
     about his teachers and how he has internalized their wisdom.
     Many of his teachers were fellow janitorial workers, cleaning
     the world to make life more comfortable for the rich and
     the middle class. He also talks about his family, his past
     experiences and frustrations in community organizing
     work and the immigrant rights movement, and of course

Black radicals who came before and are here now. And in doing so, he shows us how he is who he is through a process of bonding and sintering; and now, on the shore of the Mississippi, my ancestors and connections are here, meeting his. Every day filled with possibility, as Clifton reminds us: "everyday someone is standing on the edge of this river, staring into time, whispering mistakenly: only here, only now."

CHAPTER 15: *Gizhewaadiziwin*

106   Aaron Mills, "Miinigowiziwin: All That Has Been Given for Living Well Together: One Vision of Anishinaabe Constitutionalism" (PhD diss., University of Victoria, 2019), dspace.library.uvic.ca/handle/1828/10985; Niigonwedom James Sinclair, "Nindoodemag Bagijiganan: A History of Anishinaabeg Narrative" (PhD diss., University of British Columbia, 2013), open.library.ubc.ca/soa/cIRcle /collections/ubctheses/24/items/1.0071931.

107   Kimmerer, *Braiding Sweetgrass*.

108   Mills, "Miinigowiziwin."

109   Sinclair, "Nindoodemag Bagijiganan."

110   Native Youth Sexual Health Network, *You Are Made of Medicine: A Mental Health Peer Support Manual* (Toronto: NYSHN, n.d.), www.nativeyouthsexualhealth.com /peersupportmanual.

111   Lindsay William-Ross and Thor Diakow, "Protesters Block Intersection near Vancouver Port in Support of Jailed Indigenous Elder," *Vancouver Is Awesome*, March 3, 2021.

112   Leanne Betasamosake Simpson, *A Short History of the*

Blockade: Giant Beavers, Diplomacy and Regeneration in Nishnaabewin (Edmonton: University of Alberta Press, 2021).

113   Ibid.

CHAPTER 16: Flowing

114   Sinclair, "Nindoodemag Bagijiganan."

115   Josh also writes about this in his MA thesis, and this section is based upon his accounting of our conversation and drive. Joshua Barichello, "Relations, Not Resources: Dena K'éh as Anti-colonial Force against Yukon Wildlife Management" (master's thesis, University of British Columbia, 2024), pp. 9–12.

116   Barichello, "Relations, Not Resources."

117   "Ikwe Safe Rides: Women Helping Women," Ikwe Safe Ride website, ikwesaferide.wordpress.com/, accessed August 2, 2024.

118   Josh Barichello and Lianne Charlie, "'We Have Our Footsteps Everywhere': The Ross River Dena's Fight to Protect Dena Kēyeh/Kaska Country," *Briarpatch*, January/February 2022.

119   Barichello, "Relations, Not Resources."

CHAPTER 17: Aabijijiwan, Continual Flowing

120   Whetung, "At the Shore," pp. 16–19.

121   Olúfẹ́mi O. Táíwò, *Elite Capture: How the Powerful Took Over Identity Politics (and Everything Else)* (Chicago: Haymarket Books, 2022), p. 9.

122   I've also heard Robin D.G. Kelley say this at the virtual book launch for the book, which you can watch here: www.youtube.com/watch?v=BpLX8T6phOQ, 5:29 mark.

123 Glen Coulthard, *Red Skin, White Masks: Rejecting the Colonial Politics of Recognition* (Minneapolis: University of Minnesota Press, 2014), pp. 1–6.

124 Eva Jewell and Ian Mosby, *Calls to Action Accountability: A 2023 Status Update on Reconciliation* (Toronto: Yellowhead Institute, December 2023).

125 Victoria Gibson, "David Suzuki, Indigenous Leaders Demand Justice for Grassy Narrows," *Toronto Star*, April 19, 2018.

126 A previous version of this section was published here: "Reflecting on 20 Years since Grassy Narrows Blockade," *Rabble.ca*, December 2, 2022. And a shorter version here: "Celebrating a Tremendous—but Fragile—Victory at Grassy Narrows," *Toronto Star*, December 1, 2022, as requested by Judy DaSilva.

CHAPTER 18: *Recapturing*

127 She told a similar story here: Rhiannon Johnson, "Water Is Sacred to Indigenous People. They Have Been Fighting to Protect It for Decades," *CBC Radio*, April 22, 2023.

128 Simpson, *A Short History*.

129 Katherine McKittrick, *Dear Science and Other Stories* (Durham, NC: Duke University Press, 2021), p. 18, pp. 1–2.

130 Ibid., p. 18, p. 1.

131 Whetung, "At the Shore," p. 103.

CHAPTER 19: *Seeing the Forest from the Lake*

132 Nicole Murdock, "Sensationalizing Alleged Killers Will Not Bring Our Missing and Murdered Indigenous Women and Girls Home," *CBC News*, December 17, 2022.

133 "Community Mourns Loss of Young Woman Who 'Always Had a Heart for Everything,'" *CBC News*, May 19, 2022.

134 Ibid.

135 "Unidentified Victim of Alleged Winnipeg Serial Killer Will Be Known as Mashkode Bizhiki'ikwe or Buffalo Woman," *CBC News*, December 5, 2022.

136 Ibid.

137 See Brandi Morin's work here: Brandi Morin, "No One Is Going to Believe You," *Al Jazeera*, December 29, 2021.

138 Audra Simpson, "The State Is a Man: Theresa Spence, Loretta Saunders and the Gender of Settler Sovereignty," *Theory & Event* 19, no. 4 (2016).

139 Ibid. Also see Joanne Barker, *Red Scare: The State's Indigenous Terrorist* (Oakland: University of California Press, 2021), for her discussion of "The Murderable Indian" and "The Kinless Indian."

140 Simpson, "The State Is a Man"; and Barker, *Red Scare*.

141 Audra Simpson, "Indigenous Identity Theft Must Stop," *Emancipator*, November 17, 2022.

CHAPTER 20: *Being a River*

142 Aaron Mills also describes this in his work, relying on Elders Fred Kelley and Sherry Copenace: Aaron Mills, "Miinigowiziwin: All That Has Been Given for Living Well Together: One Vision of Anishinaabe Constitutionalism" (PhD diss., University of Victoria, 2019), p. 72.

CHAPTER 21: *Stone Canoes, Nigigoonsiwag and Seeing Through Stone*

143 There is a written version of this story in Doug's book: Williams, *Michi Saagiig Nishnaabeg*.

144 See Madeline Whetung's "At the Shore."

145 The Haudenosaunee (Iroquois) people have a profound oral and written archive of a similar being who is known in English as the Peacemaker, and they hold many different stories about his origin.

146 See Susan Hill, *The Clay We Are Made Of: Haudenosaunee Land Tenure on the Grand River* (Winnipeg: University of Manitoba Press, 2017), for her account of the Peacemaker and the Great Law of Peace.

147 Leanne Betasamosake Simpson, *As We Have Always Done: Indigenous Freedom through Radical Resistance* (Minneapolis: University of Minnesota Press, 2017), ch. 9.

148 Dr. Jessica Jacobson-Konefall, "Radiant Archives: Rebecca Belmore's At Pelican Falls," *SoundCloud*, uploaded by Platform Centre, 2021, soundcloud.com/user-58689969 /radiant-archives-rebecca-belmores-at-pelican-falls-by -dr-jessica-jacobson-konefall.

149 "The Davin Report, 1879," Nishnawbe Aski Nation

website, rschools.nan.on.ca/article/the-davin-report
-1879-1120.asp, accessed August 6, 2024.

150 For an example, see Jorge Barrera, "The Horrors of
St. Anne's," *CBC News*, March 29, 2018. For testimonials
from Pelican Falls residential school, see survivor Garnet
Angeconeb's account: Garnet Angeconeb and Ashley
Wright, "Chapter Two: Residential School," *Garnet's
Journey: From Residential School to Reconciliation* (blog),
garnetsjourney.com/chapters/residential-school/, accessed
August 6, 2024.

151 For an example, see Dirk Meissner, "Work to Exhume
Remains at Former Kamloops Residential School Could
Begin Soon, Chief Says," *CBC News*, May 20, 2022.

152 The list of students who died is from the National Student
Memorial, National Centre for Truth and Reconciliation,
University of Manitoba, and is available online: "Pelican
Lake (Pelican Falls)," NCTR website, nctr.ca/residential
-schools/ontario/pelican-lake-pelican-falls/, accessed
August 6, 2024.

153 Ian Adams, "The Lonely Death of Chanie Wenjack,"
Maclean's, February 1, 1967.

154 Ry Moran, "Truth and Reconciliation Commission,"
The Canadian Encyclopedia, September 24, 2015.

155 Al Jazeera English, "Palestinian Children Plead for
Protection in Gaza Press Conference," *YouTube*,
November 8, 2023, www.youtube.com/watch?v
=zLxHBRPLzow.

156 Sarah Wilkinson, foreword to *My Lover Was a Freedom
Fighter*, by Rana Shubair (SkyLimit Press, 2019), p. vii.
Rana Shubair, a mother, author and English teacher, was
martyred by Israeli air strikes on December 1, 2023.

157 This is from the poem "I Grant You Refuge" by Palestinian poet, novelist and teacher Hiba Abu Nada. "Refuge" was written on October 10 and is among the last pieces she composed before being martyred by an Israeli air strike on October 20. Huda Fakhreddine translated the poem from the original Arabic and you can read it here: "I Grant You Refuge," *Protean Magazine*, November 3, 2023, https://proteanmag.com/2023/11/03/i-grant-you-refuge/.

158 Mohammad El Kurd, *Rifqa* (Chicago: Haymarket Books, 2021).

159 Gumbs, *Undrowned*, p. 34.

160 For Indigenous children in Canada, that number is higher than at the height of the residential school system. Teresa Wright, "Foster Care Is Modern-Day Residential School System: Inuk MP Mumilaaq Qaqqaq," *CBC News*, June 4, 2021.

CHAPTER 22: *The One That Cleans the World*

161 Natalie Diaz, *Postcolonial Love Poem* (Minneapolis: Gray Wolf Press, 2020), p. 46.

162 Ibid.

163 Françoise Vergès, *A Decolonial Feminism,* trans. Ashley J. Bohrer (London: Pluto Press, 2021).

164 This chapter, and this paragraph in particular, was influenced and inspired by Vergès, *A Decolonial Feminism*.

165 Diaz, *Postcolonial Love Poem*, p. 46.

166 Ibid., p. 49.

167 Ibid.

CHAPTER 23: *A Theory of Water*

168 I've written a little about emergence in *Dancing on Our Turtle's Back*, but Andrea Ritchie's *Practicing New Worlds* (Chico, CA: AK Press, 2023) really lays out the importance of emergent strategies for abolitionist futures, and I'm using this language from page 85 ("fractal, adaptive, nonlinear and iterative, resilient and transformative, interdependent and decentralized, creating more possibilities") here.

CREDITS

Excerpts from "The First Water is the Body" from *Postcolonial Love Poem*. Copyright © 2020 by Natalie Diaz. Reprinted with the permission of The Permissions Company, LLC on behalf of Graywolf Press, graywolfpress.org.

Excerpts from *A Map to the Door of No Return: Notes to Belonging* copyright © 2011 by Dionne Brand. Reprinted with the permission of Penguin Random House Canada. All rights reserved.

Excerpts from *Nomenclature: New and Collected Poems* copyright © 2022 by Dionne Brand. Reprinted with the permission of The Wylie Agency (UK) Ltd on behalf of Penguin Random House Canada.

ABOUT THE AUTHOR

LEANNE BETASAMOSAKE SIMPSON is a Michi Saagiig Nishnaabeg scholar, writer, musician and artist who is widely recognized as one of the most compelling Indigenous voices of her generation. She holds a PhD from the University of Manitoba and teaches at the Dechinta Centre for Research and Learning in Denendeh. For the past two decades, as an independent scholar using Nishnaabeg intellectual practices, Leanne has lectured extensively at universities across Canada and the United States. She is also the author of eight books, including the nonfiction *A Short History of the Blockade*; the novel *Noopiming: The Cure for White Ladies*, which was shortlisted for the Governor General's Literary Award for Fiction and the Dublin Literary Prize; and the novel *This Accident of Being Lost*, which was a finalist for the Rogers Writers' Trust Fiction Prize and the Trillium Book Award. Her collaboration with Robyn Maynard, *Rehearsals for Living*, was a national bestseller and shortlisted for the Governor General's Literary Award for Nonfiction.

01 14

J